BESTSELLING AUTHOR OF
THE CRYSTAL BIBLE

JUDY HALL

ENERGY CLEANSING CRYSTALS

HOW TO USE CRYSTALS TO OPTIMIZE YOUR SURROUNDINGS

WATKINS

Sharing Wisdom Since
1893

Energy-Cleansing Crystals
Judy Hall

First published as *Earth Blessings* in the UK and USA in 2014
by Watkins, an imprint of Watkins Media Limited

This edition published in the UK and USA in 2022
by Watkins, an imprint of Watkins Media Limited
Unit 11, Shepperton House, 83–93 Shepperton Road
London N1 3DF

enquiries@watkinspublishing.co.uk

Senior Editors: Tania Ahsan and Fiona Robertson
Managing Designer: Allan Sommerville
Picture Research: Cee Weston-Baker
Production: Uzma Taj
Commissioned Photography: Michael Illas

A CIP record for this book is available from the British Library

ISBN: 978-1-78678-653-1

10 9 8 7 6 5 4 3 2 1

Printed in Turkey

www.watkinspublishing.com

Be humble for you are made of earth.
Be noble for you are made of stars.

(Serbian proverb)

Dedicated to Gaia, Mother Earth
and all those who tend and heal

CONTENTS

A MILLION CRYSTAL BUTTERFLIES

"It is time NOW for us to use the tools we have of compassion, humility and knowledge to assist one another in our personal and planetary healing journeys. How do we do this when there is so much to be done? Where do we start? Inside. We start inside working on making ourselves happier, healthier and more at peace."

John van Rees, 2011

Our world is undergoing a metamorphosis. Floods, earthquakes, tsunamis, volcanic eruptions, changes in weather patterns and pollution disasters show us that our Earth is restless and in distress. And yet within all that disharmony, the Earth has also given us tools – in the form of crystals – that can turn our thoughts and actions toward positive healing for the planet and for our selves.

This book is all about discovering these tools and learning to use them for the greater good. Many crystals have been around for millennia. Throughout this time they have constantly re-energized and restored the earth beneath our feet and the environment. In addition, some amazing high-vibration crystals have made themselves known. These may assist us not only in our attempts to heal the Earth, but also with raising our personal consciousness. All crystals can help us to create a safe, sacred space in which to live.

Our journey toward bringing balance back to the Earth begins with healing ourselves. One of the most profound ways in which you can help our planet is to work on yourself, to create your own inner peace and stabilize your well-being (I cover this in Chapter Two).

I believe that if we focus our energies on a combination of personal and Earth healing – each supporting the other, and all of us working together – we can create a shift of consciousness that really does open us up to a new reality here on Earth. Everyone can contribute to the process of realigning the Earth's own energies and healing our environment. No one person knows the best way; we all work at our own level and our own pace, and we all learn from each other. Whether you are an experienced crystal worker or this is your first experience of healing crystals, you are as much part of the solution as I or anyone else.

A while ago, following a traumatic soul-scouring that led me into deep introspection and karmic healing, I had to look at the enemy within, face my demons and draw upon deep inner strength to find my way back to my calm centre. It would have been useful at the time to have had Judy's Jasper, my Eye of the Storm stone (see page 139), which facilitates that process, but it manifested after I'd done the work myself. Nonetheless, that uncomfortable experience led me to ask some questions about the way we are in the world.

Can we find a way to pull together? A way that unites rather than divides us? Can we share what we know openly and without jealousy, honouring every contribution? Can we be butterflies dancing a new universe into being? After all, if we can't, who can?

I wrote this book to create a practical guide for a community of like-minded souls. If, as has been suggested, a butterfly beating its wings in the Amazon creates a hurricane in the Caribbean, just think how a million crystal butterflies beating their wings in unison could transform our world. Let's do it!

Crystal blessings
Judy Hall

HOW TO MAKE BEST USE OF THIS BOOK

This book is based on my many years' experience using crystals, visualizations and journeys to support the Earth and keep my personal energies high and space clear. During that time, layouts have evolved and certain crystals have become my favourites. In this book, I share these discoveries with you and suggest how you can adapt them to your own situation and landscape.

The book is intended to guide you. Along the way, I urge you to develop your intuition and to let the crystals speak to you. Open your palm chakras (see pages 24–5) and meditate quietly with a crystal before using it; allow it to communicate through your body (*sensing* the energy) or your mind (direct communication). Do not be afraid to experiment with the layouts – try different shapes and crystal combinations and learn to *feel* the energies that they each generate. Use your feet or hands to sense the direction in which energy flows, and where it is blocked – and experience how placing a crystal unlocks it. Look on it as joyful play – expand your interaction with the crystals and the Earth itself. It is my belief that in synergy, your focused intention, earth energy and the crystal's resonance create the most effective form of healing.

Crystals such as these Rose Quartzes help us to bring more love into our world.

What is crystal healing?

Crystals do not provide a "cure". Rather, crystal healing brings energy back into balance; it clears blockages and harmonizes the whole in order to restore equilibrium.

Chapter One introduces the processes of crystal creation and the basics of crystal work: cleansing and activating your crystals and focusing your intention – essential parts of the process. It shows how to open your palm chakras for the fastest download of crystal energies, and how to dowse for crystal placements. Chapter Two is all about healing you, which I believe is the only way to begin to heal the Earth. Then, Chapters Three and Four begin with basic concepts relating to the subject of each chapter, followed by specific applications of those concepts. I have included examples of how crystals have been used in real-life situations and how you can adapt layouts for your own purposes. There is a glossary on pages 156–7 to explain any terms with which you are unfamiliar.

Chapter Five is your "crystal toolkit". It contains photographs and descriptions of 30 crystals that I use for Earth healing (these are by no means all the crystals available, just those among my favourites). Some you'll find easily; others may take some hunting down – but you can always use the energy of the photographs in the book when you can't find the crystal itself. Over time you can build up your own toolkit of crystals that you find particularly effective. Keep it simple. Layouts do not have to be complex – a handful of crystals can do the job. Find the ones that work for you.

EARTH MEANINGS

Throughout this book you will see both "Earth" and "earth" – sometimes uppercase and sometimes lower. "Earth" is used to denote the name of our planet, while "earth" refers to the ground beneath our feet and the element of earth. Mother Earth is Gaia, the soul of the planet, often regarded as a divine being.

Chapter One

THE FRUITS
OF THE EARTH

Our planet is in constant dynamic motion, flowing and changing, expanding and contracting. To the ancients the Earth was alive – a living, breathing being whom they called Gaia, Mother Earth. They honoured her and the fruits of her body, the crystalline bones created by an on-going magical process of geological transformation. Precious stones were regarded as the primeval deities made manifest. Rock was immutable, incorruptible and permanent – in contrast to the frail uncertainty of human life – and it created an interface between the visible and the divine worlds.

This chapter introduces you to essential processes for working with crystals and helps you to understand how crystals formed and why they are such excellent transmitters of energy and restorers of equilibrium.

CRYSTAL CREATION

Crystals and the rocks that enfold them are reborn star matter, created and recreated by a variety of processes, each of which affects how energy is able to flow. Some crystals solidified from gases, others dripped into being and some were ground up and reformed in layers. A few were created so fast they lack internal crystalline structure. The rock on which you live, or on which a building or a sacred site is situated, has a profound effect on how energy moves through the earth *and* on your physiology. Psychogeology, the effect of geology on the mind, suggests that it may also have an effect on how you feel and experience life.

Planet Earth evolved from clouds of gases containing the minerals that constitute all life and matter on this planet. The cloud slowly condensed to form a fiery spherical globe. As this body began to cool, crystals and rocks came to life, conceived from the minerals and magma that lie between the central core and the crust. Magma – molten lava – constitutes the majority of our planet, the solidified crust of the globe being only as thin as the skin of an apple. Some minerals collected in the crust to form pockets of crystal, while others hardened into rock. Continuing processes transformed the ancient rocks.

Quartz produces electromagnetic energy fields that amplify the earth's natural energy currents. Rocks with a high Quartz content (granite, sandstone and quartzite) or metallic mineralogy (iron, copper, silver, gold) attract, conduct and amplify telluric (earth) energies creating what are known as conductive energy fields. For example, dome-shaped outcrops of granitic and sandstone conduct a synergized telluric energy in oscillating spiral patterns that culminate at the summit of the dome. Channels of rock curve sinuously around the world conveying energy. The current from Pink Granite from Aswan, Egypt, the most powerfully paramagnetic of all granites, dips under the ocean to reappear in Galveston, USA, and wend its way through the state of Texas.

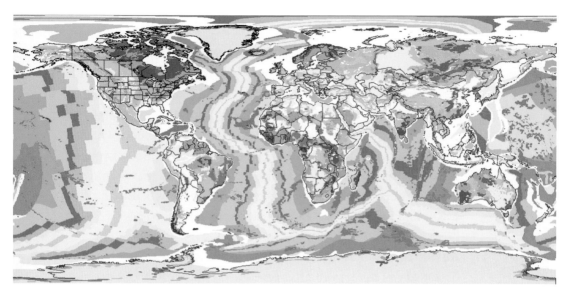

The geology of the world. Note how the lines of rock flow across continents and under oceans.

It shows itself once again in India in a gentler pink form – but the energy remains just as powerful.

Igneous rocks

Primary creations formed out of the seed material of the universe and the magma of the planet, igneous rocks are the oldest rocks of all. They are also the youngest, as the process continues today. Formed when the minerals in the primeval cosmic gaseous dust cloud condensed, or when molten lava exploded or bubbled through the Earth's crust, igneous rocks reflect the internal tensions of the globe. Holding raw primal power, the stressful process of creation imparts a powerful resonance that helps to restore stability after change and to ground energies. But first these rocks impel that change to take place, stimulating growth processes and helping to heal the past. Granite and basalt are among the igneous rocks that transmit powerful geomagnetic currents rapidly around the world. Many potent healing crystals are a result of igneous processes. When lava was expelled through faults in the Earth's crust and cooled rapidly, it created crystals such as Basalt and the Jaspers. Where the liquid magma rose up into the crust and cooled slowly in a "lake", it formed Rose Quartz and Peridot. Gaseous magma under high pressure permeated hollow rocks to create Amethyst, Tourmaline and Smoky Quartz. Aragonite, a potent Earth healer, cooled slowly in hidden vents into beautiful shapes and colours. Granite, Basalt and Smoky Quartz are particularly useful for anchoring layouts into the Earth and repairing the Earth's electromagnetic grid.

Sedimentary rocks

These are secondary rocks created from particles compressed and cemented together in layers or mixed with rainwater and dripped into being. Such particles may be the eroded remains of former igneous rock or the detritus of sea and other organic matter. Sedimentary rocks such as Limestone and Chalk are fluid and patient, allowing energy to penetrate freely. They've seen it all before and resonate with the cycles of death, decay and rebirth. However, the more claggy clays and heavy sandstones can stall energy, slowing it down, while Flint directs and grounds it along precise channels. Rhodochrosite was created through the oxidization of manganese. Stromatolite formed from alternating layers of cyanobacteria and sedimentary grains on the floor of an ocean. Recycled mineral-laden water dripped into fissures to create Selenite. These light-bearing, calming crystals assist with survival issues and riding out long cycles of time. They help you to understand the impact of your environment on your health and well-being and to let go of rigid belief patterns.

Metamorphic rocks

These are the rocks of transformation, associated with the process of mountain-building and shape-shifting as the plates of the planet push together. They were dramatically redefined when intense pressure, heat and chemical processes modified existing rock. Laid down into recrystallized plates, which in turn could be folded and bent, some of the most potent transformation crystals are found in metamorphic rocks. Metamorphic crystals include Serpentine and Jade. They help you to accept the need for change and transmutation in your life, especially the shaping and scouring that facilitates soul growth.

CRYSTAL GEOMETRY

Amorphous With no inner crystalline structure, an amorphous crystal such as Obsidian allows energy to pass rapidly through.

Cubic With axes at right angles to each other, cubic crystals such as Halite are grounding and stabilizing, facilitating reorganization.

Monoclinic Created from parallelograms that pass energy smoothly, monoclinic crystals such as Selenite assist with purification.

Triclinic Asymmetric triclinic crystals such as Feldspar assist with energy integration and focus.

Orthorhombic With different length axes, orthorhombic crystals such as Aragonite efficiently cleanse and stabilize energy.

Tetragonal Rectangular tetragonal crystals such as Rutile absorb and transmute energy, bringing balance and resolution.

Trigonal With a triangular internal lattice, trigonal crystals such as Quartz generate, store and radiate energy.

Hexagonal Created from three-dimensional hexagrams, hexagonal crystals such as Rhodochrosite maintain equilibrium.

Quartz is one of the most common crystals in the world and takes many forms.

Quartz

The most common crystal, Quartz is the bones and brain cells of Mother Earth and the Quartz family contains some of the highest vibration crystals yet known. Quartz may be found in metamorphic rocks but is not a result of the metamorphic process. Quartz was formed when fiery gases given off by igneous processes in the magma cooled and solidified, or were heated or dripped upon and continued to grow. Its highly organized internal crystal lattice not only efficiently passes energy through itself, but generates and stores it as well, making Quartz useful for slow-release healing. The speed of cooling and the minerals incorporated into the process dictate the specific shape and precise form that the Quartz, or any other crystal, takes.

The crystal lattice

A crystal is defined by its internal structure – an orderly, repeating atomic lattice. Owing to chemical impurities, radiation, earth and solar emissions, and the exact means of their formation, each type of crystal has its own specific energy signature and lattice. A crystal is symmetrical along an axis. Each matching pair of faces in the lattice has exactly the same angles. The internal structure of any crystalline formation is constant and unchanging. It is this alignment that allows energy to pass through a crystal and resonate with the energy fields that surround it. While a number of crystals may form out of the same mineral or combination of minerals, each type crystallizes out differently. It is the *internal* geometry of a crystal, not the external shape, that determines the crystal's type and action.

CRYSTAL BASICS

It's tempting to rush straight into the healing work, but you can make your crystal experience much more productive if you look at the basics first. For example, crystals carry the energy of everyone who touches them, so many draw off toxic vibes and all require regular cleansing. Crystals want to cooperate with you, so setting an intention is vital. And, finally, there is one small secret – palm chakras – that makes your crystal work so much more potent.

Choosing your crystal

There are a number of ways in which you can choose your crystals – see dowsing and opening the palm chakras later in this chapter. Intuition is another way: simply pick up the one that feels right to you. You may also find that your hands, or feet, tingle when you pass your palm over or hold the right crystal, or that one sticks to your hand when you run your fingers through a tub. There is no one crystal perfect for any of the exercises in this book, there is only the crystal that is right for you to work with at that moment.

Love and intention

Working with focused intention and unconditional love really amps up crystal energies and makes best use of their potential. Simply hold the crystal for a few moments before commencing work and state your intention. Phrasing your intention in the now is much more potent than projecting it into the future. Say "my intention is that so and so happens" – not "will happen", which pushes your intention into a future that may not manifest. When placing your crystals, do so with love and a clear intention.

Dedicating, cleansing and recharging your crystals

Before beginning your crystal work, and after it is finished, you need to cleanse your crystals as they quickly pick up negative energies. Their energies may have been damaged by the means of their collection. Mining through blasting shocks their etheric body just as it would ours. Spending time helping your crystals to settle down and restore their energy when you first acquire them is a prerequisite to them being fully available for healing work. Cleanse them, place them on an already regenerated Quartz or Carnelian, leave them out in the sun or under the moon, and give them time to recover. Tell them how special they are, how much you appreciate being a caretaker for them, and ask them to join you in the important work of Earth healing – beginning with their own birthplace. If they are badly shocked, a proprietary crystal recharger can be helpful (see Resources, page 158).

If the crystal is not friable, soluble or layered, you can cleanse it simply by placing it under running water – although preferably not tap water – for a few moments. Dry the crystal and place it in the sun if it has been depleted or shocked. Or, you can add a drop or two of proprietary crystal cleanser to a spray bottle of spring water and spray the crystal lightly with this – this works for friable and soluble crystals, too. Alternatively, place the crystal overnight

Placing your crystal on a large Quartz, Carnelian or Citrine cluster cleanses and recharges it.

in uncooked brown rice. As salt can damage friable or layered crystals it is better avoided as a cleansing agent but you could place the crystal in a bag with several pieces of Halite overnight. Smoky Quartz also cleanses crystal energies, but the Quartz itself requires cleansing in due course. The sun recharges a crystal as does placing it on a large Quartz or Citrine cluster, but you can also use a proprietary recharger.

Once you have cleansed and recharged your crystal, take a few moments to dedicate it to the highest good of everything that comes into contact with it, including the Earth itself. Simply hold the crystal in your hands and state out loud:

"I dedicate this crystal to the highest good of all. May healing flow to all who come into contact with it, especially the Earth."

How do I know when the healing is complete?

You need to establish your own signals – and could finger dowse for this (see page 23). You'll probably find that you feel a rush of energy while the healing is taking place and that this rush gradually subsides or suddenly cuts off as the healing is complete. Once the flow of energy stops, remove the crystals – or leave them in place if you are doing Earth healing through direct placement or on a map. Remember to cleanse them when the work is done.

LAYOUTS

The specific pattern in which you place your crystals is called a layout. These can be either geometrically closed layouts, such as a Pentangle (see page 46) or radiating layouts, such as a Sunburst (see page 51).

DOWSING

Dowsing establishes exactly where a crystal should go in a layout or a space, or on a map. It also helps select the right crystals. If you are looking for an energy line in a space, dowsing rods will twitch and cross as you find the line. You can also "body dowse" with your palm chakras or the bottom of your feet – your body tingles as though a current is running up your arms or legs.

To pendulum dowse

- Hold your pendulum with the chain wrapped loosely around your hand and about a hand's breadth of chain hanging down.
- To establish "yes" and "no", hold the pendulum over your knee and ask: "Is [state your name] my name?" The pendulum swings in a circle (note direction of swing) or backward and forward. This is your yes. Repeat using a false name, this is your no. For a "maybe", the pendulum may shimmy a little or move sluggishly.
- Once you have established yes and no, ask "Is this the right crystal?" and/or "Is this the correct place?"

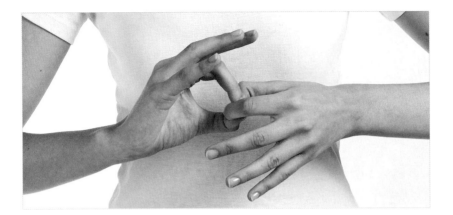

To finger dowse
- Loop the thumb and first finger of one hand together.
- Place the thumb and finger of the other hand through the loop and close.
- Ask your question and pull firmly. If the loop holds the answer is yes; if it pulls apart the answer is no.

To dowse with rods
- Hold the rods loosely, one in each hand pointing forward. Step forward slowly. The rods swing inward and cross over or outward as you reach a vortex or energy line. With practice, you can use your yes and no movements to establish whether you have reached an earth energy or a water line, and so on.

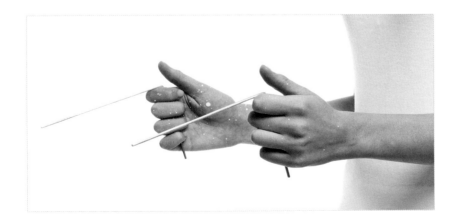

SENSING THE PALM CHAKRAS

The palm chakras are energy centres in the palms of your hands. Opening them enables you to *sense* crystal energies and to channel healing. Like all chakras, the palm chakras both receive energy and radiate it out. When these chakras are open, you absorb energy from the universe, the Earth or your crystals. This energy flows into your energy field and you can channel it out again as appropriate. The chakras lie in the centre of your palms, but the energy radiates out to your fingertips as well as up your arms. When the palm chakras are open and active, it is as though there is a ball of pulsating energy between your palms.

To open the palm chakras

1   Keeping your fingers loosely bent, put your fingertips together, palms facing, heels of your hands apart.

2   State your intention to open the palm chakras. Then, "rock" each hand so that first your heels touch (fingertips separate), then your fingertips come back together (and your heels separate). Repeat this rocking motion five or six times.

3   Move your hands away from each other and focus your attention on your right palm and then your left. (Or, left then right if you are left-handed.) Picture the chakras opening like petals, and becoming hot and energized.

4   Bring your hands toward each other again. Stop when you feel the energy of the two chakras meeting. (With a little practice, you'll be able to open the chakras simply by thinking about opening them.)

To close the palm chakras

When you have finished your crystal work, wash your hands or fold your fingers inward to close the palm chakras.

CRYSTAL PROTOCOL

Crystals are living beings worthy of respect and layouts are potent energetic matrixes that we need to create and maintain carefully. When working with crystals or layouts remember:

- Cleanse your crystals before and after use, and also cleanse the space around them. Do not blow on crystals to cleanse them as your energies may not be pure. Use spring water or a proprietary crystal cleanser.

- Ask permission from guardians and higher beings before placing a layout, especially at or near sacred sites. Create your layout in harmony with the Earth's needs, not those of your ego.

- Dowse or ask for the highest possible guidance as to which crystals are suitable for a particular layout. Circumstances change with each layout and the person placing the crystals.

- Layouts pick up and amplify negativity, so avoid idle chatter or toxic thoughts; remain positive.

- Once you have released a toxic energy, do not speak of it again. To do so re-anchors it, making your work pointless.

- Deconstruct layouts when your work is complete, or hold the intention that only that which is for the highest good remains.

CRYSTAL POINTS

Crystal points channel energy in the direction they face. Open your palm chakras and hold the pointed end of a crystal on your palm. Feel the energies radiating into you. Lay the crystal flat and turn the point toward your wrist. Feel the energy flow up your arm. Turn it away from you and sense the flow change. Crystal clusters radiate energy in all directions at once.

Chapter Two

PERSONAL
ENERGY CARE

In order to help the Earth, we must first look after our own
physical body, and (importantly) our own subtle energies.
Staying calm, protected and centred in your body puts you in
the best "space" to help others. Having a filter system in place
to ensure that only beneficial energy reaches you means
that you function more effectively in your everyday world. You
can achieve all this if you keep your chakra system cleansed
so that it is working optimally. There is a power source – the
dantien (see page 29) – that you can call on to boost your
overall healing ability and raise your own energy level. And
there are additional chakras that you can open up to assist
your connection with higher dimensions and the Earth.

KEEPING YOUR OWN ENERGIES CLEAR

Like the Earth, our bodies have a subtle energy system that enables us to function effectively on many levels when it is healthy and in balance. This system comprises the chakras, the endocrine glands and the body's subtle energy meridian systems. If negative energies, toxic thoughts or repressed emotions pervade the subtle energy system, dis-ease results.

Accentuate the positive

Your thoughts create an energy field that may be positive and constructive or negative and destructive. If you want to heal the Earth, avoid toxic thoughts – and toxic people. If you constantly focus on the negative or on fear, that is what you attract. Keeping your thoughts focused on the positive is one of the simplest ways to keep your own energy clear and also that of the space around you. Building a positive energy field keeps subtle energies high and enables you to emit positive, healing thoughts for the Earth.

Holding a Carnelian over your dantien recharges your energy.

Wear a crystal programmed to protect your energies from invasion from toxic people (hold the crystal with this intention): Black Tourmaline, Smoky Quartz or Brandenberg are ideal. Cleanse the crystal thoroughly each evening.

The powerpoint: the dantien

A small, slowly revolving sphere about two fingers breadth below your navel, the dantien links to the autonomic nervous system and sits atop the sacral chakra. This is where power – or Qi – is stored in your body. If the dantien is empty or depleted, your creative energy cannot function and you feel ill at ease. The dantien may be drained if you use your own energy during healing rather than channelling that of the crystals or if people or places draw on your energy. Tape crystals over your dantien to nourish and activate it, or place your hands over it and breathe deeply into it. Amplify your dantien's power by holding a highly energetic crystal, such as Carnelian, Golden Healer or Bumble Bee Jasper, over the spot.

The dantien provides an anchor that connects you to the earth. Before commencing Earth healing, stand for a few moments with your feet slightly apart and knees relaxed and somewhat bent, and your hands over your dantien. Consciously make a connection from the dantien across to your hips, down each leg and out through your feet to the root and earth star chakras beneath. Here the connections twine together in a cord that goes deep down into the earth to anchor itself at the planet's core. Earth energy can travel up this cord and healing energy can go down through it.

CRYSTAL SHIELD

Hold a protective crystal such as Black Tourmaline or Purpurite on your palm chakra. Feel the crystal energy growing large until it envelops you in a big bubble. Picture the edges of this bubble crystallizing so that you are within the crystal. Wear the crystal to remind you of your protective shield.

HARMONIZING THE PSYCHE

A lemiscate (figure-of-eight) layout placed on and around your body purifies and harmonizes your psyche, gently grounding you and bringing together your mind, emotions, body and spirit. This layout is particularly helpful if you find events in the outside world disturbing – it restores your equilibrium, calming you so that you can take remedial action and set healing in motion.

THE LEMISCATE LAYOUT

Crystals: Preseli Bluestone; Golden Healer, Golden Herkimer or Golden Quartz; Smoky Elestial or Smoky Quartz

A lemiscate draws energy downward from the highest source and upward from the earth, synergizing the two. You can achieve this synergy with only three key crystals placed as shown. If you wish, add further high-vibration crystals (see pages 148–53) above your waist to raise your consciousness, and earthy vibration crystals (see pages 136–47) below it to fully anchor the harmonized energy.

1   Choose a time and place in which you will not be disturbed.
2   Hold the crystals in your hands, stating your intention that they harmonize your psyche and calm your mind.
3   Sit down with your legs out in front of you and with enough space behind you so that you can lie down. Place the Smoky Elestial or Smoky Quartz below and to the left of your feet.
4   Now lie down. Place the Golden Healer, Golden Herkimer or Golden Quartz over your dantien.
5   Place the Preseli Bluestone above and to the right of your head.
6   Visualize a figure of eight going from the Preseli Bluestone round and down through the golden stone, crossing over and moving down to the Smoky Quartz, then returning up the

For an instant cleanse, sweep a piece of Anandalite™ from your feet up to your head, over your head and down your back returning to your feet. For instant calm, hold a Rose Quartz or an Eye of the Storm over your heart.

other side. (You could also ask a friend to do this connection for you using a crystal wand.)

7   Lie quietly for ten to 15 minutes or until you no longer feel the energy moving around the lemiscate. Allow the energy to settle itself into a shield around you – this shield filters the energies you pick up from the external world.

8   Sit up slowly. Remove the crystals in the opposite order to the one in which you laid them. Feel the energetic shield around you. Stand up and feel your feet connecting with the earth.

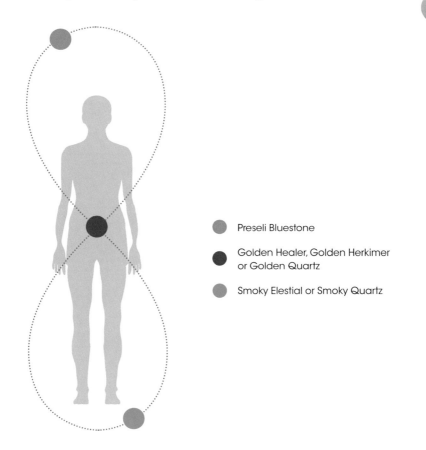

● Preseli Bluestone

● Golden Healer, Golden Herkimer or Golden Quartz

● Smoky Elestial or Smoky Quartz

THE EVERYDAY CHAKRAS

Your chakras provide a filter between your inner energies and the energies of the outside world. Cleansing them is essential if you are to carry out personal, space or Earth healing effectively.

The chakras link the physical body with the subtle energies of the etheric body. They keep the physical and subtle bodies in harmony. To an intuitive eye, they spin and whirl, and blockages show up as dark spots or as "wobbles" as each chakra turns.

In crystal healing we often use the body's seven major chakras (see diagram), plus the root (earth) chakra beneath your feet, which keeps you gently grounded and helps you to sense the energy of place. The table opposite lists each of the everyday chakras, its position, function and associated crystals. This table can help you when choosing which crystals to use in a healing.

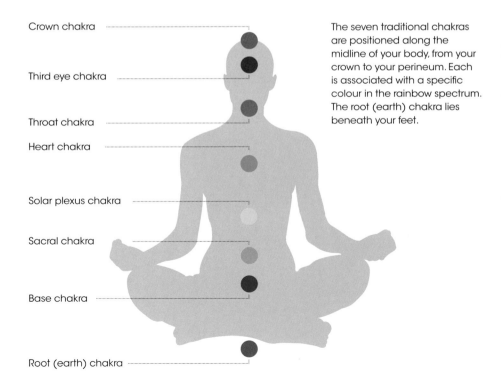

Crown chakra

Third eye chakra

Throat chakra

Heart chakra

Solar plexus chakra

Sacral chakra

Base chakra

Root (earth) chakra

The seven traditional chakras are positioned along the midline of your body, from your crown to your perineum. Each is associated with a specific colour in the rainbow spectrum. The root (earth) chakra lies beneath your feet.

EVERYDAY CHAKRA CLEANSING LAYOUT

Crystals: Dowse, intuit or draw upon the traditional chakra-colour associations (see below) for appropriate stones. Or, place Halite over each chakra for a fast cleanse and Golden Healer for a rapid recharge. Cleanse the crystals before you begin.

1   Lie down comfortably in a place where you will not be disturbed. Hold your crystals in your hands and state your intention that they cleanse and rebalance your chakras.

2   Place a Smoky Quartz or other appropriate crystal between and slightly below your feet. Picture energy radiating out from the crystal into the root (earth) chakra for a minute or two. Become aware that the chakra is being cleansed and its spin regulated. Leave the crystal in place.

Layout continues overleaf ▶

The everyday chakras

Chakra	Position	Function	Crystal
Root (earth)	Beneath the feet	Grounding and protection	Flint / Smoky Quartz
Base	Perineum	Energizing and survival	Malachite / Menalite
Sacral	Below navel	Creating and activating	Bumble Bee Jasper / Tangerine Dream
Solar plexus	Above navel	Nurturing, feeling	Citrine / Golden Healer
Heart	Over heart	Healing emotional distress, radiating love	Rose Quartz / Rhodochrosite
Throat	Adam's apple	Communication, expressing yourself	Golden Herkimer
Third eye	Centre of forehead	Metaphysical attunement and inner sight	Anandalite™ / Preseli Bluestone
Crown	Top of head	Opening intuition and higher awareness	Selenite / Spirit Quartz

3   Place a suitable crystal on your base chakra. Picture energy radiating out from the crystal into this chakra, as before.

4   Place an appropriate crystal on your sacral chakra, just below your navel, and again feel the cleansing process.

5   Repeat for the remaining chakras: place an appropriate crystal on your solar plexus, heart, throat, third eye and crown chakras in turn, each time feeling the cleansing process.

6   Lie still for a few moments and feel the crystals re-energize your chakras and this energy radiate through your being.

7   When you're ready, move your attention slowly from the soles of your feet up the midline of your body, feeling the balance and harmony of each chakra as your attention reaches it.

8   Gather your crystals, starting at the crown. As you reach the root chakra, be aware of a cord anchoring you to the earth.

9   When you have finished, cleanse your stones thoroughly.

OPENING YOUR ROOT CHAKRA

This simple exercise instantly connects you to the planet. Use this exercise whenever you begin a healing session to maximize healing energy and keep you grounded.

Focus on the soles of your feet. Breathe deeply, into your toes. Slowly exhale. Imagine that you have a root growing from each of your feet into the earth. Below your feet the two roots twist together to form one strong bond. Where they meet is your root (or earth) chakra. This root goes on down into the earth, passing through the stone beings who breathe only every 100 years or so. It passes through the fiery molten magma that powers the planet, until finally it anchors itself around a huge crystal at the centre of the Earth. This root holds you gently in incarnation. When your root chakra is open, energy can pass up it to you and you can send energy down it to the Earth.

THE INTERMEDIARY CHAKRAS

Two little-known chakras – the spleen chakra and the past-life chakra – can radically affect how well your energies function.

Spleen chakra

Positioned under the left armpit, the spleen chakra is the place where energetic hooks lodge from "psychic vampires" – needy people who wittingly or unwittingly pull on your energies. In balance, this chakra is self-motivated and full of power.

Past-life chakra

Found behind the ears along the bony skull ridge, this chakra offers wisdom, skill and instinctive knowing. It is also where your own unfinished business, unfulfilled promises, emotional baggage and ingrained beliefs cause energetic interference. Restoring this chakra to pristine functioning speeds up the opening of the high-vibration chakras (see page 36).

INTERMEDIARY CHAKRA CLEANSING

To cleanse the spleen chakra, position Eye of the Storm, Green Aventurine, Green Jade or Bloodstone a hand's breadth under your left armpit. Wind the crystal anticlockwise to pull out energetic hooks. Lay the crystal flat against the chakra to heal and seal it.

To cleanse the past-life chakras, massage along the ridge of your skull with your crystal (Brandenberg, Stromatolite, Kambaba Jasper, Preseli Bluestone or Golden Healer) or fingers. Place one crystal behind each ear and one at the base of your skull. Hold the intention that the crystals dissolve the negative effects of the past.

THE HIGH-VIBRATION CHAKRAS

High-vibration chakras act like higher octaves of the basic chakras. They open up to connect you with multi-dimensions and expanded consciousness and are usually activated with high-vibration stones. Open and cleanse one higher chakra at a time, allowing it to settle in before opening the next. When you have finished a healing, close your chakras: if the higher chakras are left open, they can be subject to subtle interference that can hamper your attempts to deal with the everyday world. When they open and close appropriately, these chakras harmonize the energetic vibrations for positive effects. (At times they open spontaneously.)

Earth star chakra

Position: below the feet beyond the root chakra

Quality: material connection

Positive effect: grounding, practical; helps you to operate well in reality and connect to the soul of the planet

Negative effect: ungrounding; causes you to pick up negativity easily, or become overly influenced by spirits of place, lost souls or traumatic events

Regulating crystals: Aragonite, Black Tourmaline, Elestial Smoky Quartz, Eye of the Storm, Flint, Granite, Halite, Rhodozite, Smoky Quartz

Heart seed chakra

Position: base of the breastbone

Quality: reminds you that you are an eternal soul

Positive effect: connecting you to the divine plan; raising awareness of the reason for your incarnation; enables you to manifest potential

Negative effect: feeling rootless, purposeless or affected by outdated unfinished or karmic business; leaves parts of your soul in other lives or dimensions

Regulating crystals: Anandalite™, Brandenberg, Eye of the Storm, Perumar™, Rhodochrosite, Rose Quartz

Higher heart chakra

Position: midway between the heart and the throat

Quality: unconditional love

Positive effect: makes you more forgiving, accepting, spiritually connected and autonomous

Negative effect: increases spiritual disconnectedness, grief and neediness; you feel overly attached to guides and mentors and influenced by "lost souls" or "walk-ins" who take over your physical body

Regulating crystals: Anandalite™, Eye of the Storm, Spirit Quartz

Soma chakra

Position: above the brow, at the hairline

Quality: spiritual connection

Positive effect: you feel more spiritually aware and fully conscious of your soul connection

Negative effect: cuts you off from spiritual connection

Regulating crystals: Herkimer Diamond, Preseli Bluestone, Purpurite, Trigonic Quartz

Soul star chakra

Position: above the head

Quality: spiritual enlightenment or illumination

Positive effect: gives you the ultimate soul connection and an objective perspective on the past; mystical awareness, humanitarian service

Negative effect: brings spiritual arrogance, soul fragmentation or a messiah complex (using your power to control others); you may feel overwhelmed by ancestral or other spirits

Regulating crystals: Anandalite™, Brandenberg, Spirit Quartz, Tangerine Dream Lemurian, Trigonic Quartz

Stellar gateway chakra

Position: above the soul star

Quality: cosmic doorway to other worlds

Positive effect: offers you multi-dimensional access and expanded consciousness; enables communication with enlightened beings

Negative effect: disintegration; you are open to cosmic disinformation and unable to function in the world

Regulating crystals: Anandalite™, Brandenberg, Fire and Ice, Trigonic Quartz

Alta major chakra

Position: inside the skull

Quality: cosmic consciousness

Positive effect: activates your lightbody that carries expanded consciousness and connects to multi-dimensional worlds

Negative effect: holds ancient and ancestral memories that may be projected onto others in the current life; the chakra may contain memories of the traumatic disintegration of former civilizations

Regulating crystals: Anandalite™, Green Ridge, Golden Healer, Herkimer Diamond, Preseli Bluestone, Purpurite, Rainbow Mayanite, Smoky Elestial, Trigonic Quartz

Note: Activating and clearing this chakra may well bring up old angers and resentments. However, you need to feel, acknowledge and let these go so that you can anchor a new energy frequency here on Earth.

Before undertaking any healing work, consciously open the higher chakras. (If you are clearing a past life in a particular place, you'll need to open the past-life chakra – see page 35 – too.) When you have finished the healing, close the chakras again, but leave the earth star open as an anchor that keeps you grounded.

HIGH-VIBRATION CHAKRA LAYOUT

Carry out this layout in small stages until you have cleansed, regulated and opened all the higher chakras, and you have control over them. Dowse or use your intuition to choose which of the regulating crystals to use. Cleanse your crystals before you begin.

1   Lie down in a place where you'll be undisturbed. To activate the earth star, place one of its crystals 12in (30cm) or so below your feet; for your heart seed chakra, place a crystal at the base of your breastbone; and to activate your higher heart chakra place one of its crystals between your physical heart and your throat.
2   Feel the three-chambered heart chakra opening and integrating as the heart, heart seed and higher heart merge.
3   To activate the soma chakra, place a stone on the centre of your hairline where it meets your brow. Open the soul star by placing a regulating crystal point downward above your head.
4   To activate the stellar gateway, reach as far as you can above your head and place one of its crystals point downward.
5   Finally, to open the alta major, place a crystal in the hollow at the back of your skull, or one on either side of your skull.
6   Lie quietly allowing the energies to shift and fizz as they cleanse and activate the higher chakras.
7   Practise opening and shutting the chakras so that they come under your conscious control. You could do this simply by picturing flower petals opening and closing. However, at first, you may need to remove a crystal and place your hand over the spot in order to close that chakra down.

Chapter Three

SPACE CLEARING AND ENERGY ENHANCEMENT

If your healing work is to have the best results, your own energy and that of the space in which you live and work need to be clean and "high". That way, you can safely expand your awareness, connecting not only to the earth energies beneath your feet, but also to higher-frequency inter-dimensional energy. Crystal layouts are particularly useful for maintaining your energetic space. The grid that each layout creates draws in energy so that it can be transformed before it is radiated out again into the surrounding space. Altars can also help to create sacred space in which to live and work. In this chapter you will find layouts that help you to raise the vibrations around you, as well as useful techniques for dealing with noisy neighbours, "sick" buildings and other, similar problems with space.

THE LAYOUTS

Placing stones in geometric layouts creates an energetic grid that cleanses, protects and energizes a space. The simplest way to grid a room or other space is to place a crystal in each corner. However, over the following pages, you'll find other useful layouts to try.

Creating a layout circuit

Every layout makes an energy "circuit" that radiates energy. In most layouts, especially those that are geometrically closed (such as a triangle or a star), the lines of force in the energy circuit (or grid) need to join together so that they completely enclose a space, without any breaks. In other words, the lines must have an uninterrupted connection. So, if the space that you want to heal means that the lines of force have to pass through walls or solid objects, use a crystal wand or the power of your mind to connect the grid.

If an alignment has a long axis, after laying out the grid check that the axes are straight. For small layouts, use a ruler;

SACRED GEOMETRY

Sacred geometry is based on natural forms, harmonious relationships and the recognition of innate patterns. The ancient Greeks believed that God created the universe according to an underlying geometric plan. They believed that geometric shapes represent the basic patterns of existence and possess extremely potent, universal energies. We can utilize these energies for space clearing and Earth healing. Sacred geometry opens up new resonances and energy frequencies and it reminds us that we are part of a sacred whole. The ancient Hermetic maxim "As above, so below; as within, so without" operates within nature and within the universe. If you can heal a small part – especially yourself – you bring the whole into balance.

for larger ones, use a broom handle (see photograph below). Adjust the crystal positions if you need to, until you have perfect alignment. Radiating layouts, such as the Spiral (see page 49), are not closed and are set in motion by intention. (Remember that crystal points channel energy in the direction they face, so position your crystals so that they point to the next spot on your layout.)

Deconstructing a layout

When a layout has completed its work, take it down in reverse order. Spray the space with a proprietary crystal cleanser, burn a joss stick, or sprinkle salt or Halite. Some energy patterns are very potent, particularly if you made them using high-vibration stones. To further deconstruct these, drum or clap out the energy, holding the intention that only what is for the highest good remains. I find Tibetan tingshaws or Petaltone Zl4 essence the most effective tools for deconstructing high-vibration grids. You can leave some energetic imprints in place as they can continue to be beneficial. Dowse or use your intuition to check if this is so.

A broom handle or a photograph can help you to check the alignment of a large layout (if you're using a photograph, beware of any camera distortion). This grid needed adjustments.

TRIANGULATION LAYOUT

FUNCTION **Establishes boundaries, protective, cleansing**

You need only three crystals for this layout, forming a triangle with a crystal at each point. Triangulation works well to protect positive energy, to neutralize negative energy and to bring in positive vibes. The energy radiates out of both sides, and above and below the geometric figure. Place one crystal in the centre of a wall or space, and the other two on the wall or space opposite, creating equal angles, if possible. Connect the three points with a wand or the power of your mind to strengthen the grid.

44

A crystal on each point of a triangle creates a multi-dimensional stabilizing grid. These are Eye of the Storm.

STAR OF DAVID LAYOUT

FUNCTION **Protective, transmuting, attracts and locks in energy**

Consisting of two interlocking triangles, the Star of David layout is traditionally used for protection. It is excellent for neutralizing ill-wishes (Black Tourmaline is a brilliant crystal to use for this). Lay the first triangle point downward to lock energies in, and join up the points with a wand. Lay another triangle point up over the top to draw down beneficial energies. Join up the points. Cleanse the star daily (see pages 19–21). Reverse the process to draw in beneficial energies to an area, before locking them in.

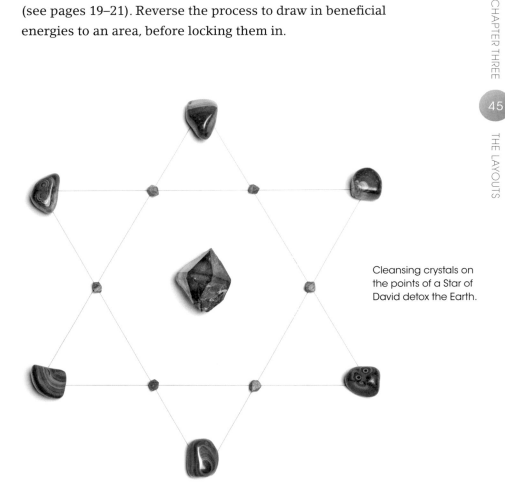

Cleansing crystals on the points of a Star of David detox the Earth.

PENTANGLE LAYOUT

FUNCTION **Space-clearing, protective, enhances energy**

A pentangle or five-pointed star is drawn with a continuous energy line. It is particularly useful for working on maps, and it also provides protection and space clearing, calls in love and healing, and can enhance your energy or the energy of a site. Follow the direction of the arrows on the diagram when placing crystals and remember to complete the circuit back to point 1 when joining up the layout with a wand. The pentangle layout can also be inverted to draw energy down into an area.

Aragonite and Rhodozite help to energetically clear and stabilize the Earth.

ZIG-ZAG LAYOUT

FUNCTION **Cleansing, stitches energy
sites together**

A series of open triangles, a zig-zag layout is an efficient
way in which to cleanse the energy of a space. It is particularly
useful to heal areas with sick building syndrome or environmental
pollution, but it also stitches energy sites together, joining them
up. Place your crystals as shown on the diagram below. You can
use one type of crystal, such as Black Tourmaline or Smoky Quartz
to absorb energetic toxicity, or you could alternate your chosen
crystal with crystals such as Selenite to bring in light. Cleanse
this layout regularly (see pages 19–21).

Selenite above Smoky
Quartz purifies a space.

LEMISCATE LAYOUT

FUNCTION **Integrating, draws energy down from above and up from below**

The Lemiscate (figure-of-eight) layout draws spiritual energy down into a site and synergizes it with earth energy to create perfect balance. Put a suitable stone at the centre of the lemiscate. Place high-vibration stones above the centre point to the crown and back down to the central stone. Place grounding stones below. You can space out the stones equally and put them opposite each other, but they may be more potent when they are offset, as this subtly alters the energetic net. Complete the circuit, joining up the figure of eight back at the first stone you placed.

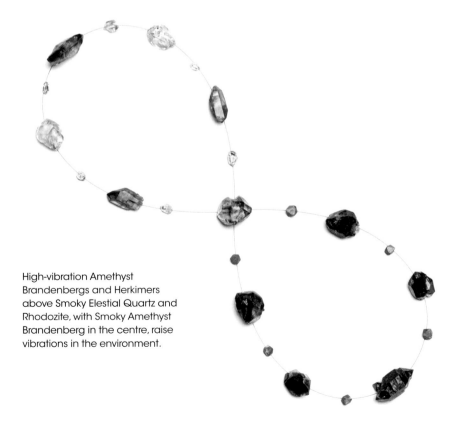

High-vibration Amethyst Brandenbergs and Herkimers above Smoky Elestial Quartz and Rhodozite, with Smoky Amethyst Brandenberg in the centre, raise vibrations in the environment.

SPIRAL LAYOUT

FUNCTION **Re-energizing, cleansing, radiating**

Depending on which way you place it, a spiral draws energy down into the centre (if you place a crystal at the top of the spiral to begin) or radiates it out (if you place a crystal at the centre first). Dowse or use your intuition to check whether you should be using a clockwise or an anticlockwise spiral and how many crystals you need. When completing the circuit (see pages 42–3), do not join the ends by going back to the first crystal you laid – spiral the energy out and away or down into the centre. You could also use a multi-armed spiral (see page 109).

Crystals placed point-downward
in a spiral draw energy to the
centre of the layout.

FLOWER OF LIFE LAYOUT

FUNCTION **Unifies, radiates healing energy**

The Flower of Life includes templates for the five Platonic Solids: primal patterns that occur within crystals – and everywhere. To the ancient Greeks, these solids symbolized the elements of fire, earth, air, water and spirit (or ether) respectively. This layout is called the Flower of Life because it encompasses the building blocks of life in one perfect form. The Flower of Life is useful as a background for layouts as the drawn pattern and the crystals work together to radiate healing energy worldwide.

Crystals can be placed on the Flower of Life in any pattern that feels right for your purpose.

SUNBURST LAYOUT

FUNCTION **Radiates energy**

A radiating sunburst energizes a whole area. It is
particularly useful to energize the Earth via a map
but you can also lay it out on the ground (see pages 97–9)
or bury it within it if your layout is to be a permanent feature.
Although it is usual to begin this layout in the centre and work
outward, you may find it helpful to dowse for your placements –
for example, you may need to set out a central alignment first, or
place crystals to draw in energy. You can always adjust the layout
to fine tune the energies. You do not need to complete a circuit of
this layout, as the intention is to radiate the energy outward as
widely as possible.

Tangerine Dream Lemurians around a Golden Herkimer radiate energy out into
the environment.

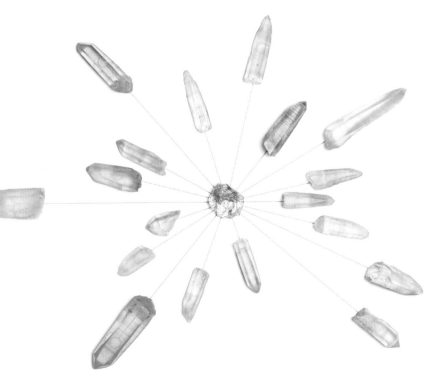

CRYSTAL LAYOUTS IN YOUR HOME

Layouts do not have to be large, covering a whole area, to be effective. You can place small crystals in protective and cleansing layouts such as the Triangulation, the Pentangle or the Zig-zag, or in energizing layouts such as the Spiral or the Sunburst, in even the smallest spaces at home.

Some high-vibration crystals can be expensive, so in a small layout use only one of these in the centre and add clear Quartz points facing away from the centre to amplify and channel the energy outward. You can leave these layouts in place for long periods, but do cleanse them frequently. If the space is polluted by electromagnetic smog or geopathic stress, use the darker-coloured earthy crystals or Herkimer Diamonds. If the pollution is from subtle radiation, try Malachite in a zig-zag formation. Bright crystals such as Citrine have the advantage of attracting abundance into your home, and Rose Quartz brings in more love.

Single-stone remedies

If your space is very limited, you can keep the energies in your home (or at work) clean and clear by placing just one large crystal – such as Elestial Quartz, Herkimer Diamond or Selenite – close to the entrance door. This purifies all energies entering your space and fills the place with light. The stone needs regular cleansing (see pages 19–21) so that it can continue to absorb negative energy and transmute it into beneficial vibes.

NOISY NEIGHBOURS REMEDY

To help quieten noisy neighbours, place a large piece of Rose Quartz against the adjoining wall or between the properties.

CLEARING AND PROTECTING TRIANGLE

Suitable crystals: Black Tourmaline, Eye of the Storm, Flint, Graphic Smoky Quartz, Halite, Herkimer Diamond, Smoky Quartz

1   Cleanse your crystals and fill them with intention.
2   Place a small crystal midway along one wall or one side of your space.
3   Place similar stones in the corners on the opposite side.
4   Join up the triangle with a wand or the power of your mind.

Note: If triangulating a whole house or apartment, place one stone by the entrance door and the other two in the corners of the farthest boundary wall opposite that door. Join the lines with your mind if they have to pass through walls.

SUNBURST

Suitable crystals: Bumble Bee Jasper, Citrine, Clear Quartz, Fire and Ice (in the centre), Golden Healer, Herkimer Diamond, Lemurians, Selenite, Rose Quartz, Tangerine Dream.

1   Choose a place where the layout will not be disturbed.
2   Cleanse your crystals and fill them with intention.
3   Lay the central stone, then lay radiating "arms". Allow your intuition to tell you how many arms and in which directions, or follow the compass directions. Picture light and energy radiating out from the layout throughout your space.

Try it now
Crystals: whichever you choose
Create the layout best suited to your needs at this moment.
Sense its effect on your space in an hour, in a day and in a week.

ALTARS TO ENHANCE ENERGY

Setting up a crystal altar does not mean that you are worshipping the crystal. Rather, the altar brings divine, sacred energy into your home and dedicates your space. It gives you a focus to be thankful for the blessings you receive, which in turn enhances the energy in your home. In addition, an altar can be a tool for meditation, during which you send out healing.

Choosing a location

You can set up an altar inside your home or outside among nature. First, though, you will need to decide whether you want to create a personal altar that is a quiet retreat from the world for you, or whether you want to share your altar with others. If the altar is to be personal, use a room that you save for quiet study or contemplation, or a corner of your bedroom. If you prefer your altar in a shared space, choose somewhere where it will be protected from children and pets – or anyone else who might pick up the crystals. If your altar is intended for Earth healing, the garden or in front of a window may be most appropriate.

Setting up your altar

Choose a cloth for your altar – find something that has an appropriate texture and colour. Lay out the cloth and position a large, central crystal on it to give your altar a focal point. Spend a few moments focusing on the intent and purpose of the altar. If you have space, it is better to have several altars dedicated to different purposes; but if you have room for only one, "all-purpose" altar, think about the different intentions it has and choose and group crystals appropriately.

Add sets of crystals dedicated to each specific purpose, such as bringing in love, healing the Earth and so on (see pages 55–6 for ideas). If you wish, add candles, an offering bowl, fresh flowers, photographs, shells, feathers, written affirmations or treasured objects – but keep the altar uncluttered and harmonious. You could add a statue of a deity, especially if that deity represents a quality such as compassion or wisdom, or is meaningful to you.

Once your altar is complete, spend a few moments contemplating its harmony. Welcome in the crystal devas (see page 87), holding the intention that they work with you to achieve your aims. Dedicate your altar to the highest good, as well as to your specific purpose (or many purposes if your altar is all-purpose). Try to spend a few moments in front of your altar each day.

ALTARS FOR SPECIFIC PURPOSES

Altars can be simple affairs – say, just one crystal – or more complex energy-generators. Here are some suggestions to help you set up and dedicate a crystal altar in your home or garden.

Earth-healing

You can dedicate this altar to sending healing energy wherever it is needed in the world.

Suitable crystals: Eye of the Storm, Graphic Smoky Quartz, Halite, Menalite, Rhodozite, Shiva Lingam, large Smoky Elestial, Smoky Quartz

Balancing the elements

Dedicate this altar to strengthening and balancing the five elements throughout the natural world.

Suitable crystals (by element type):
Earth: Brown Aragonite, Eye of the Storm, Flint, Graphic Smoky Quartz, Menalite, Rhodozite, Shiva Lingam, Smoky Elestial Quartz, Smoky Quartz

Air: Fire and Ice, Herkimer Diamond, Lilac Aragonite, Preseli Bluestone, Selenite

Fire: Bumble Bee Jasper, Citrine, Granite, Lemurian, Rose Quartz, Tangerine Dream

Water: Blue Aragonite, Clear Quartz, Halite, Stromatolite, Trigonic Quartz

Ether (Spirit, or Above and Below): Brandenberg, Fire and Ice, Rainbow Mayanite, Spirit Quartz, White Aragonite

Honouring the ancestors

Dedicate this altar to bringing resolution and peace to your ancestral line.

Suitable crystals: Perumar™, Preseli Bluestone, Rhodochrosite, Smoky Spirit Quartz, Stromatolite

Fertility and abundance

Dedicate this altar to bringing more fertility to the earth, and creativity and abundance into your life and the lives of those around you.

Suitable crystals: Bumble Bee Jasper, Citrine, Golden Healer, Kambaba Jasper, Lemurians, Menalite, Shiva Lingam, Stromatolite, Tangerine Dream

Radiating love and peace

Dedicate this altar to sending love and peace throughout the world.

Suitable crystals: Anandalite™, Eye of the Storm, Perumar™, Rhodochrosite, Rose Quartz, Selenite

CRYSTALS IN THE WORKPLACE

As you probably spend a great deal of time at work, it makes sense to use crystals to enhance your working environment and ensure that the energy there is as high and as pure as possible. Crystals can also improve relations with your colleagues. Overall, they can absorb negative vibes, create a less stressful atmosphere, assist with problem solving, improve communication and counteract electromagnetic pollution.

Where can I put my crystal?

On your desk, on a nearby window ledge, in a drawer, taped under a table or put discreetly in a corner are all good placements – crystals work even when hidden behind a filing cabinet. If you have room, create a layout. Do not be concerned about your colleagues' reactions. Most people instinctively respond to the "good vibes" a crystal puts out.

How can crystals help me at work?

Many jobs require problem solving. Crystals help you to combine careful analysis with an intuitive solution – looking at things from a different perspective. They can activate talents you did not know you possessed. Tourmaline aids lateral thinking, analyzing difficulties and finding a conclusion. Tourmalinated Quartz, or a

CRYSTAL SOOTHERS

Keep a small bowl of tumbled stones around – either for yourself or for other people to "play" with. Their soothing properties soon make themselves felt! Remember to cleanse them regularly.

combination of Tourmaline and clear Quartz, dissolves crystallized patterns and harmonizes disparate elements.

If your job means that you have to deal with difficult people or situations, or complaints, keep a Black Tourmaline close to you – tape one to your phone or wear it around your neck. It absorbs verbal or psychic attack and keeps your energies safe.

If you work in an environment with combative, competitive energy, use a crystal ball, which transmutes that energy to make it more productive. Crystal balls can also help in environments with chaotic and fragmented energy, helping everyone to pull together. Rose Quartz can calm quick tempers; Spirit Quartz, or a Clear Quartz cluster, brings harmony and clarity of purpose that encourages straightforward decision-making.

If you work as part of a team, a large Spirit Quartz facilitates compromise and cooperation between members, improves communication (helping to overcome bickering or internal criticism) and assists with reaching your goals. A Smoky Quartz draws off negative energies and helps resolve conflict, as does Eye of the Storm. Rose Quartz is useful for softening *attitude*.

If you find it difficult to express your ideas, hold a Citrine or a Shiva Lingam. If you find it difficult to accept constructive criticism, keep an Aragonite in your pocket. This crystal calms over-sensitivity and helps you to see the cause of the problems.

Overcoming electromagnetic stress

Created by computers, phones and other gadgets, electromagnetic stress often exacerbates discomfort and disharmony within the workplace. Place a crystal next to a computer, tape one to your phone, or grid your space with a crystal layout to transmute the negative energy and help you to function more productively.

Suitable crystals: Black Tourmaline, Flint, Herkimer Diamond, Preseli Bluestone, Smoky Quartz, Shungite

HARMONY IN THE WORKPLACE LAYOUT

Crystals: Clear Quartz, Rhodochrosite, Rose Quartz, Selenite

The Flower of Life layout (see page 50) is particularly useful for bringing harmony into the workplace. If you don't have anywhere to place this layout at work, lay it out at home and hold the intention that the positive vibes go to your workplace.

1   Draw or print out a Flower of Life mandala. If you are creating the layout at home, place it over a picture of your workplace.
2   Cleanse your crystals (see pages 19–21) and dedicate them to bringing harmony into your workplace.
3   Place the first stone in the centre of the mandala.
4   Pick up the next stone and intuitively place it on the Flower.
5   Space your crystals equally around the Flower to form a harmonious pattern. Stop only when the layout feels active, peaceful and complete.
6   Leave the layout in place for as long as possible, but remember to cleanse it regularly.

SICK-BUILDING SYNDROME

A building with air pollution or inadequate ventilation, excess static electricity, electromagnetic smog, geopathic stress and the like may suffer from "sick-building syndrome". The effects on you might include lack of concentration, headaches, chest and skin problems, nausea, excessive fatigue and dizziness. Use the Zig-zag layout on page 47 to heal the building – and yourself.

CRYSTAL FENG SHUI

Feng Shui is the ancient Chinese art of harmonizing the energy of space. Crystal Feng Shui uses crystals to direct energy flow through your home (or other space) to attract and generate beneficial energy and to overcome energetic blockages or whirlpools. Highly polished crystals, including crystal spheres, reflect energy across a space and can turn it around corners. Some systems of Feng Shui rely on compass directions, and others on direction from the front entrance, to create the *bagua* (see illustration, below).

The houses of life

In Feng Shui, placing appropriate crystals in certain areas of your home is believed to transform the part of your life that corresponds to that particular room in the house, or position in the room. (It is particularly auspicious to place a crystal in both the relevant room of the house and the corresponding position in the relevant room.) To work out your *bagua* (which parts of your house relate to which areas of your life), orient your house from the front door (or the door by which you usually enter) and map out the house

WEALTH & PROSPERITY		LOVE & RELATIONSHIPS
FAMILY & PHYSICAL HEALTH	SPIRITUAL HEALTH & WELL-BEING	CHILDREN & CREATIVITY
KNOWLEDGE & WISDOM	CAREER	TRAVEL & HELPFUL PEOPLE

In this *bagua*, the front door is in the career area of life.

Area of life	Suggested crystals
Self-knowledge/wisdom	Brandenberg, Clear Quartz, Fire and Ice, Selenite
Career/life mission	Anandalite™, Bumble Bee Jasper, Selenite, Stromatolite
Travel/helpful people	Anandalite™, Malachite, Trigonic Quartz
Children/creativity	Bumble Bee Jasper, Citrine, Golden Healer, Rose Quartz
Spiritual well-being	Citrine, Eye of the Storm, Herkimer Diamond
Family/Health	Anandalite™, Rhodochrosite, Golden Healer, Spirit Quartz
Prosperity/self-worth	Citrine, Golden Herkimer
Fame/reputation	Kambaba Jasper, Purpurite, Spirit Quartz
Love/relationships	Shiva Lingam, Menalite, Rose Quartz

according to the diagram opposite. Clear Quartz in the health area generates health and well-being; Malachite in the same position attracts helpful friends. Citrine in the wealth corner generates abundance. Choose your own Feng Shui crystals from the table above, or select them intuitively, and place them in your home. Use the largest crystals you have and cleanse them (see pages 19–21) regularly. Monitor the difference in the energy of your rooms over the course of a month and try new combinations, if appropriate.

You can also place appropriate crystals in specific rooms. For example, if your toilet is placed in the wealth corner, although you may attract money into the house it will continually be flushed away. Placing a large Citrine geode on or near the cistern solves the problem.

Feng Shui and colour

Traditionally Feng Shui uses colour to influence specific areas of life. You can place crystals of an appropriate colour in areas of the house that correspond to the relevant section of the *bagua*. So, for example, if you want to "grow" your career, red crystals in the career area just inside the front door will give your career a boost, yellow could bring a better salary and orange could make you more creative in your career choice. Use the table below to guide your selection of crystal colours.

Crystal spheres

Polished, highly reflective crystals, spheres are useful for slowing energy down or speeding it up in a particular space. They absorb stagnant and negative energy and radiate a harmonious, calming energy, and of course they reflect the shape of our globe.

Depending on your needs and situation, place the crystal sphere in an area that requires more harmony and light and an influx of fresh energy. For example, if there are constant disagreements in a house, a large clear Quartz sphere placed in the main living room neutralizes negative emotions and gives more clarity on situations. Alternatively, a Smoky Quartz grounds energies and defuses tension, while an Eye of the Storm sphere in the centre of the house creates an aura of calm throughout. Try a Rose Quartz sphere to create a gently soothing, loving and nurturing energy – especially excellent in a child's room or a bedroom. A Citrine ball can assist in overcoming money worries.

FENG SHUI CRYSTAL COLOURS

- **Red**: growth and energy
- **Orange**: creativity and increased libido
- **Green**: wisdom, intellect and entrepreneurship
- **Yellow**: wealth
- **Blue**: peace and health
- **Purple**: spiritual advancement

In general, you can place crystal spheres:

- where there is chaotic energy, such as in a small hallway with many doors (place as close to the centre as possible by a wall so that the energy can flow smoothly around the sphere).
- in the front window of a house that faces a road or stands on a corner (which means that dagger-like energy strikes the house), to divert the energy.
- in a long, narrow and dark hallway (place at the end of the hallway to reflect back the light).
- in a dark corner or dead end to avoid a build-up of stagnant energy and draw in light.
- halfway down a set of rooms that open out of each other to slow the rapid energy flow from room to room.
- at the top of the stairs if the stairs lead immediately up from the front door so that energy reaches both floors equally.
- near or outside the front door or corner of the house if a road sweeps past, carrying rushing energy with it.

Crystal spheres are excellent tools for smoothing out energy flow.

Chapter Four

ENVIRONMENTAL HEALING

Our planet is a vast, living, breathing bio-organism far greater than its physical size. It is part of an enormous eco-system that spreads out across space. In ancient times, the Earth was regarded as a divine creation and crystals were its bones, water its blood, the forests its lungs. Ancient people were aware that the Earth contained supercharged areas that they regarded as sacred. In this chapter we look at ways to maintain the Earth's energetic biosphere and to restore harmony to our planet's energy and chakra grid, as well as to its trauma sites and disturbed places. Earth healing ceremonies or crystal layouts on leylines, or at the chakras and other vortex points, can open, purify, align and heal the Earth's energy field and promote overall global well-being.

THE EARTH'S ENERGY AND CHAKRA GRID

The Earth has a subtle, interpenetrating grid of lines of energy that link the vortexes and chakras around the globe. When these energy lines are operating properly, they create a complex but harmonious geometric pattern. However, if they intersect inappropriately, conflict, or are disturbed or distorted, they can create disequilibrium – or "hot spots"– that may need to be healed. How do you know you're on an energy line? Your hands or feet tingle and a dowsing rod or pendulum quickly confirms the flow.

The global matrix grid

Just as the physical body has an etheric counterpart that is linked to and mediated by the chakras, so does the Earth. A complex meridian matrix with a strong energy field surrounds and interpenetrates the Earth's own "subtle body". The result is a system of intersecting energy lines – some geomagnetic, others electromagnetic; some telluric, others cosmic – that form a global grid flowing with powerful currents.

Magnetic lines attract, electro lines stimulate and energize, and electromagnetic lines activate and attract. Ancient peoples had an innate understanding of these telluric energies (which could perhaps be described as the Earth's nervous system). They built stone circles, temples and other significant structures, "inserting" them into the grid at intersections to activate, amplify, regulate, harmonize and ground the energy flow. The material most often chosen for these structures was stone with a high Quartz content.

Mythographer and geomancer Paul Broadhurst describes the Earth's grid not only as an energy grid, but also a carrier of ancestral memories and elemental energies. It is for this reason, he argues, that it is so potent as a healing tool:

Intersecting force lines grid the globe. If the pattern remains stable and in harmony, well-being results.

"Each place is linked by a vast spreading network of natural channels that run through the Earth, like the nerves of a gigantic body. The race memories, the myths and spirit of ancient people are still alive in them, waiting to be triggered when they can unleash powerful images of renewal and transformation. Certain sites are especially adapted by nature to be the focus of specific elemental forces, each with its resonant effect on the human mind."

We could call the energies that pass through this grid the Earth's Qi or life force. The health and well-being of the Earth – and that of everything living on her – depends upon the healthy flow of this Qi. If the grid is broken or blocked in any way, especially by geopathic stress or the intrusive activities of humankind, the environment suffers and the beings who inhabit the affected area feel out-of-sorts, disconnected and unnourished.

Along the lines of the global matrix grid lie the Earth's chakras and meridian lines. There is no consensus as to exactly where these are located, but everyone agrees that Earth healing is facilitated by harmonizing or diverting the lines to bring the global matrix grid back into equilibrium. Natural electromagnetic energy lines – the Hartmann Net, the Curry Grid and similar geopathic lines – radiate out all around the globe creating powerful forcefields. These lines may not always be in harmony, particularly where they intersect or interact with significant landscape features or manmade structures such as electricity pylons, buildings or quarries, as this distorts them to create areas of intensified radiation. Research has shown that these "knots" of energy, called geopathogens, can have a detrimental effect on health, interfering with cell metabolism. Suitably placed crystals can deflect or absorb the resulting geopathic stress, bringing conflicting energy currents back into equilibrium to energetically transform a space. You can place the healing crystals at the actual intersection or on a map – the energy fields entrain no matter where in the world you are.

The vortexes

Vortexes are powerful energy spots at sites such as Lake Titicaca in Bolivia/Peru, and Sedona, Arizona, USA (which has more energy vortexes than any other place on Earth). Vortexes are like acupuncture points on the subtle meridian lines of the Earth. These spiral eddies may flow clockwise or counterclockwise. They may flow outward, spiralling energy up from the earth (an electrical vortex), or pull inward, drawing energy from above into the earth (a magnetic vortex). Some vortexes are a combination of electromagnetism – "a vortex within a vortex" – that has both an inward and an outward flow. Disturbances and blockages in the

THE ELEMENTAL VORTEXES

Experts have identified four vortexes, located at certain sites on Earth, which are each associated with an Element (see pages 55–6 and 104)and drive the whole energy grid.

Earth – Table Mountain, Cape Town, South Africa

Air – Great Pyramid–Mount of Olives

Fire – Haleakala Crater, Hawaii

Water – Lake Rotopounamu, North Island, New Zealand

vortexes cause dis-ease elsewhere in the system, but you can also use them to balance energy and restore equilibrium to the system either at the actual site or through placing crystals on a map.

Earth's major chakra system

Sometimes covering huge areas, the Earth's major chakras each radiate out from a central sacred site. For example, Glastonbury, in southwest England, is the Earth's heart chakra.

Additional Earth chakras are becoming active to assimilate higher vibrational energies and experts have now identified more than 156 of them altogether. Dobogoko in the Pilis Mountains, Hungary, for example, is the heart chakra of that country, but it also has an "upgrading" effect. Together with the Ganges in India, it boosts the depleted energy of Glastonbury and opens a three-chambered heart chakra just like the one that occurs in the physical body when the heart seed and higher heart chakras are activated and take the heart chakra to a new vibration (see page 37).

THE SEVEN MAJOR EARTH CHAKRAS

The following seven Earth chakras and their locations make up the "major" chakra system of the globe.

Base chakra: Mount Shasta, California (alternatives: Grand Canyon, Sedona, Black Mesa, all in the USA)

Sacral chakra: Lake Titicaca, Bolivia/Peru (alternatives: Machu Pichu, Peru; Amazon River, South America)

Solar plexus chakra: Uluru, Australia

Heart chakra: Glastonbury, England (alternatives: River Ganges, India; Dobogoko, Hungary)

Throat chakra: Great Pyramid, Egypt

Third eye chakra: Kuh-e Malek Siah, Iran (alternative: Mount Fuji, Japan)

Crown chakra: Mount Kailash, Tibet

THE MINOR EARTH CHAKRAS

Just as with the chakra systems of the human body, many minor chakras support the major Earth chakras. The following is a list of the locations of the Earth's minor chakras as identified by geomancer Robert Coon who has been researching them for almost 50 years.

Africa

Dakar, Senegal
Fogo, Cape Verde Islands
Great Zimbabwe Ruins, Zimbabwe
Isangila Falls, Democratic Republic of Congo (Zaire)
Jebel Toubkal, Morocco
Kaalom, Lake Chad, Chad
Kgalagadi Transfrontier Park, Botswana/South Africa
Lake Victoria, Tanzania/Uganda
Mont-aux-Sources, Lesotho, South Africa
Mount Dimlang, Shebshi Mountains, Nigeria
Mount Loma, Sierra Leone
Mount Nkungwe, Tanzania
Pico de Teide, Tenerife
Pilansberg, South Africa
Shott el Djerid, Tunisia
Table Mountain, Cape Town, South Africa
Timbuktu, Lake Faguibine, Niger River, Mali
Tsodilo Hills, Botswana
Uhuru Peak, Kibo, Kilimanjaro, Tanzania

Antarctica

Bear Island
Elephant Island
Mount Hope, Eternity range
Prydz Bay
Sanae area
South Pole

Arctic Circle

Lake Thingvallavatn, Thingvellir, Iceland
Nuuk, Greenland

Asia and India

Adam's Peak, Sri Lanka
Arunachala Hill, Chennai, India
Kuh-e Malek Siah, Zahedan, Iran
Mecca, Saudi Arabia
Mount Damavand, Iran
Piram Island, Narmada River, Gujarat, India
Sundarbans–Sagar Island–Great Banyan Tree, Botanic Garden, Kolkata, India/Bangladesh
Takht-e Soleyman, Iran

Atlantic Ocean/Caribbean

Ascension Island
Graciosa, Azores
Great Exuma Island, Bahamas
Montego Bay, Jamaica
Port Stanley, Falkland Islands
Somerset Island, Bermuda
South Georgia
St George's Island, Bermuda
St Helena

Australia and New Zealand

Adelaide Peninsula, Australia
Blue Mountains, Australia
Fraser Island, Queensland, Australia
Hamelin Pool, Gathaagudu (Shark
    Bay), Western Australia
Lake Rotopounamu, New Zealand
Mount Picton, Tasmania, Australia
Nourlangie Rock, Kakadu, Northern
    Territory, Australia

Europe and Russia

Brandenburg Gate, Berlin, Germany
Callanish, Isle of Lewis, Hebrides,
    Scotland
Chersky, Siberia
High Tatras, Poland/Slovak Republic
Independence Fjord, Greenland
Karakul Lake–Ismail Samani, Pamirs,
    Tajikistan
Klyuchevskaya Sopka, Kamchatka
    Peninsula, Russia
Lake Baikal, Russia
Lake Balkash, Kazakhstan
Lake Ozero Taymyr, Siberia
Lena–Muna junction, Siberia
Lisbon, Portugal
Longyearbyen, Spitsbergen
Montserrat–Placa de Catalunya,
    Barcelona, Spain
Mount Elbrus, Caucasus, Republic
    of Georgia
Mount Konzhakovsky Kamen, Central
    Ural Mountains
Mytikas, Mount Olympus, Greece
Sakhalin Island, Poronaysk, Russia
Sergiev Posad–Danilov, Moscow,
    Russia
Stortorget, Gamla Stan, Stockholm,
    Sweden
Tunguska, Russia

Vozrozhdeniya Island, Aral Sea,
    Uzbekistan/Kazakhstan
Yuzhny, Novaya Zemlya, Russia

Far East, China and Indonesia

Angkor Wat, Cambodia
Borobudur, Java, Indonesia
Emei Shan–Gongga Shan–Leshan
    Buddha, Sichuan, China
Hall of Supreme Harmony, Beijing,
    China
Karakorum, Gobi Desert, Mongolia
Khao Nan Mia, Surat Thani, Thailand
Lake Toba, Sumatra, Indonesia
Mani San, Ganghwa Island, North/
    South Korea
Mount Belukha, Mongolia
Mount Fuji, Japan
Mount Kinabalu, Sabah, Malaysia
Mount Pulag, Luzon Island,
    Philippines
Po Lin (Precious Lotus) Monastery,
    Lantau Island, Hong Kong
Sefa Utaki, Nanjo City, Okinawa
Snow Mountains, Papua, Indonesia
Tai Shan, Shandong Province,
    China
Tirta Empul, Bali

Indian Ocean

Big Ben, Heard Island
Morne Seychellois, Victoria, Seychelles
Mount Maromokotro, Massif de
    Tsoratanana, Madagascar
Mount Ross, Kerguelen Islands

North and Central America

Akimiski Island, James Bay, Canada
Bay of God's Mercy, Southampton
    Island, Canada

Boulder, Colorado, USA
Cahokia Mounds, Illinois, USA
Cascada Cola de Caballo–Cerro de la
    Silla–Fuente de la Vida,
    Monterrey, Mexico
Cerro de Puntas, Puerto Rico
El Tule–Palenque, Mexico
Fox Islands, Aleutian Islands, Alaska,
    USA
Golden Hinde, Strathcona Provincial
    Park, Vancouver Island, Canada
Great Bear Lake, Canada
Halifax, Nova Scotia, Canada
Kachina Peaks Wilderness,
    Arizona, USA
Laguna Corcovado, Corcovado
    National Park, Costa Rica
Mount McKinley, Alaska, USA
Mount Whitney, Death Valley,
    California, USA
Niagara Falls, USA/Canada
Pilot Knob State Park, Iowa, USA
Washington DC, USA
Wood Buffalo National Park,
    Alberta, Canada

Pacific Ocean

Haleakala Crater, Hawaii
Hivaoa Island, Marquesas Islands
Kiritimati, Kiribati
Macquarie Island
Mauna Loa–Mauna Kea, Hawaii
Mount Lamlam, Guam
Mount Orohena, Tahiti
Mount Panié, New Caledonia
Mount Silisili, Western Samoa

Mount Tomaniivi, Fiji
Mount Simpson–Mount Victoria, Papua
    New Guinea
Nan Madol, Pohnpei, Micronesia
Pihemanu (Midway Atoll/Islands)
Piton des Neiges, Reunion Island
Popomanaseu, Guadalcanal,
    Solomon Islands
Rano Aroi, Easter Island
Rano Koi, Easter Island
Snow Mountains, Papua New Guinea
Tarawa Island, Gilbert Islands
Yap Island

South America

Angel Falls, Venezuela
Corcovado Mountain, Rio de Janeiro,
    Brazil
Iguazu Falls, Argentina/Brazil/
    Paraguay
Lago Arari, Ilha de Marajo, Brazil
Lake Buenos Aires, Argentina
Marco Zero–Praca da Republica,
    Fazenda Nova, Brazil
Parnaiba River Headwaters, Piaui,
    Brazil
Peter and Paul Rocks, Brazil
Plaza de Armas, Santiago, Chile
Plaza de Mayo, Buenos Aires,
    Argentina
Plaza Mayor, Lima, Peru
Praca dos Tres Poderes, Brasilia, Brazil
Rio Ucayli and Rio Maranon
    confluence, Iquitos, Peru
Teatro Amazonas, Brazil
Terreiro de Jesus, Salvador, Brazil

LEYLINES

Lines of power carrying earth electricity, leylines consist of ancient alignments of above-ground features of ceremonial and cultural significance that reflect an energy path below. Telluric energy tends to flow along natural paths of conductive mineralogy, such as Quartz or metal-rich rocks, or may follow underground water courses. Leylines are often sinuous and intertwined with male and female polarity currents running alongside each other. Contrary to popular belief, they are not necessarily straight – they may comprise triangles and other geometric figures.

For example, the longest leyline in England is the Michael and Mary line, which passes from St Michael's Mount at the tip of Cornwall through Glastonbury and Avebury to exit at Hopton on the Norfolk coast. It has many intersecting lines radiating off it.

Standing on a leyline can be like plugging into the electricity mains. Some people are particularly susceptible to leyline energies and to the geopathic stress they may generate. Leylines can become blocked and toxic with "energy sumps" that suck in and hold negative energy. Clearing this flow is an essential part of Earth healing. Judicious placement of crystals can, to some extent, manipulate and direct leylines around any obstacles.

Sun and moon lines

Some sacred sites have 12 "sun" lines radiating out from a central point. These lines correspond to the signs of the zodiac as they occur along the ecliptic (the sun's path through the heavens). The sun's movement overhead charges up the lines, which become particularly powerful at the solstices and equinoxes. The same site may well have 13 "moon" lines, too. These store and hold the energy of the yearly lunation cycle. Placing appropriate crystals along them can recharge the energies of an area (see pages 97–9).

HOW DOES EARTH HEALING WORK?

I wish I had a coherent, scientific answer to this question, but I don't! I do know that intention and resonance play a part, as do frequency and vibration. I have insights gained from quantum physics, but I am not a physicist; and from brain neurology, but I am not a neuroscientist. Nor am I am a geologist. However, a lack of scientific understanding doesn't prevent us from exploring how energy and consciousness function in a holistic universe, where everything is connected to everything else; in other words, in a unified field. Here's a quick summary of the main theories.

Electromagnetism

At its simplest Earth healing has it roots in electromagnetism. As with our bodies, Planet Earth has electromagnetic and other telluric currents running through it. It is postulated that the tiny electromagnetic energies that crystals generate can influence the currents flowing in the earth. The crystals' currents bring earth currents back into harmony in the same way that acupuncture needles harmonize the physical and subtle bodies.

Quantum physics: riding the crest of a wave

The 20th-century theoretical physicist Burckhard Heim put forward the Quantum Field Theory. This postulates a universe on four levels and in six dimensions, rather than the previously scientifically accepted four.

That there are more dimensions is something crystal healers experience on a daily basis. Quantum physics suggests that quantum particles can inhabit any or none of the various levels and dimensions simultaneously. It hypothesizes that energy is not continuous, but exists as "packs" – energy that behaves like separate particles and yet can act like a wave. The quantum particles transfer information patterns over great distances and time, which explains why crystals can work at a distance.

In discussing consciousness and quantum physics in 1987, US theoretical quantum physicist Dr Fred Alan Wolf suggested that consciousness was a huge oceanic wave washing through everything. He pointed out that everything is composed of this "froth" and that we would see ourselves under an electron microscope as, "a rather bizarre-looking light show, of things popping on and off, vanishing and reappearing, matter created out of nothing before vanishing again. And in that vanishing and creation, an electromagnetic signal is piped from one point to another point." This is exactly what happens within a crystal as it interacts with the Earth and its energy field. Here are some other principles of quantum physics that resonate with Earth healing:

- Only one thousandth millionth part of our body is matter. The rest is energy.
- Photons control matter. In other words, energy controls matter.
- Fundamental particles, such as electrons, protons, neutrons, photons and neutrinos, can influence each other at a considerable distance – a concept known as "non-locality".
- Everything is interconnected in such a way that the properties of the smallest pieces contain the properties of the whole.
- "In some strange sense the quantum principle tells us that we are dealing with a participatory universe." (Professor John Wheeler, UK)
- One quantum particle can be in two places at once.
- Quantum particles come into existence when observed.

Entrainment

As bundles of energy, crystals can affect their environment – this comes about through entrainment. In Earth healing entrainment is defined as a sympathetic resonance between two energy fields. Time and distance, and size, have no relevance here. A crystal's pulsing energy field has perfect equilibrium and its sympathetic resonance stabilizes a larger field through energetic synchronization especially when directed by intention. Entrainment is used to send healing and restore balance to a specific site or to the Earth's matrix grid through the placement of crystals on maps and diagrams. These energetically transfer harmony to the larger energy field, which can be considered to be a holographic universe.

The holographic universe

A hologram is a system in which a part contains the information of the whole. US theoretical physicist David Bohm conceived the notion that the parts were actually organized by the quantum whole and had the property of non-locality – that is, they did not exist in time and space.

The notion that information contained within a hologram is non-local explains why a crystal in one part of the world can resonate or entrain with another or with an energy field anywhere. In a hologram one tiny fragment contains the whole folded within until it is projected out to the world.

We could look on the crystal world as a holomovement – each individual crystal carrying a dynamic imprint of the whole. In a hologram, we can access any part of the whole if we shine a laser through it at any point. In Earth healing, intention replaces the laser – shining light to access global energy within the crystal.

Scalar waves

It is my belief that healing work is the result of scalar waves. These are found throughout the universe and within our physical bodies. Bioscalar wave energy (that is, scalar energy within living matter) exists at the microscopic level in the nucleus of an atom or a cell or the building blocks of a crystal. It creates a bioenergetic source more powerful than DNA, cellular matrixes and other physiological processes. It activates the meridians and facilitates healing at the energetic interface between spirit and matter.

It is probable that all healing crystals have this energy within their matrix, and that their crystalline structure actually produces bioscalar energy that might operate on the human and planetary energy body, stimulating the ability to self-heal. The depiction of the energetic pattern of scalar waves is remarkably similar to how an intuitive eye perceives the energies radiating out from a crystal or the energy patterns surrounding the Earth (see page 66–8).

Bringing it all together

If the body, the brain and the consciousness are inextricably linked with all other matter in the universe and can entrain, we are connected by an invisible network (scalar waves) to each and every thing in that universe – including crystals and the Earth itself. Through the frequency of our thoughts and intention we can

Golden and Clear Selenite generate massive amounts cf bioscalar waves.

affect the whole, particularly when we amplify the entrainment through the resonating energies of a crystal. Heal the subtle energetic etheric level, bring it back into balance, and the physical will follow.

EVERYDAY FIVE-MINUTE EARTH-HEALING

Crystal: Selenite

1 Find somewhere quiet to sit where you will be undisturbed. Open your palm chakras, then close one hand around your piece of Selenite, holding the crystal lightly in your palm.
2 Imagine you are holding Mother Earth and that the Selenite is filling the whole Earth with white light.
3 Once the image of the Earth is filled with light, visualize the Earth's matrix grid lighting up. In your mind's eye, see a strong protective shield around the outer edges of the Earth's biomagnetic field. Hold this thought for up to five minutes and then put your crystal down, disconnect from the matrix grid and stand up, ensuring you are properly grounded.

Selenite radiates crystallized divine light.

THE SOLSTICES AND EQUINOXES

Countless cultural traditions mark the winter and summer solstices, auspicious days since ancient times. Solstices are precise astronomical moments that vary in timing and date (see below). Prehistoric sacred sites were aligned to frame sunrise or sunset on the winter or summer solstice. Because Earth's orbit is tilted, the north–south position of the sun, as viewed from the Earth, changes as the Earth moves annually around the sun. On a solstice the sun is at its greatest or nearest distance from the equator and at its highest or lowest position in the sky, creating the longest and shortest days. The equinoxes occur midway between at the points when day and night are of equal length.

The word "solstice" comes from the Latin for "the sun stands still". For a few days before and after the solstice, the sun appears to rise or set in the same spot. In the northern hemisphere, the sun stays closer to the horizon during the winter solstice than at any other time of year, yielding the least amount of daylight. In the southern hemisphere the December solstice marks maximum daylight. Here the winter solstice is celebrated in June, the time when the northern hemisphere celebrates the summer solstice. You can use the solstice or equinox moment, or sunrise or sunset, to time your rituals to harness the potent power of the sun to your Earth healing.

DATES AND TIMES OF THE ASTRONOMICAL SOLSTICES AND EQUINOXES

	Equinox	Solstice	Equinox	Solstice
2014	20 Mar 16:57 GMT	21 Jun 10:51 GMT	23 Sep 02:29 GMT	21 Dec 23:03 GMT
2015	20 Mar 22:45 GMT	21 Jun 16:38 GMT	23 Sep 08:20 GMT	22 Dec 04:48 GMT
2016	20 Mar 04:30 GMT	20 Jun 22:34 GMT	22 Sep 14:21 GMT	21 Dec 10:44 GMT
2017	20 Mar 10:29 GMT	21 Jun 04:24 GMT	22 Sep 20:02 GMT	21 Dec 16:28 GMT
2018	20 Mar 16:15 GMT	21 Jun 10:07 GMT	23 Sep 01:54 GMT	21 Dec 22:22 GMT

IN THE FOOTSTEPS OF OUR ANCESTORS – SACRED SITES AND EARTH ENERGY

A place of palpable power, a sacred site is a threshold between worlds. For as long as there have been human beings, there has been sacred landscape, dotted with particular sites that resonate with our deepest selves and compel us to interact with the divine. These sites were often situated among stunning natural features or placed at points of geo-energetic significance on the Earth's chakra system. Powerful vectors and generators, they literally powered the landscape.

Sacred sites are surrounded by a powerful radiating energy field, rather like a magnet. They have naturally strong earth energies created by geomagnetism, geoelectricity, leylines, underground water, telluric or dragon currents and so on.

Coming home

Evolving over thousands of years, and sometimes changing their orientation, sacred places weren't just decoration on the landscape. They were an integral part of ancient cosmology. All sites are multi-experiential and multi-layered. In older times the gods interpenetrated everything and, for the most part, sacred sites were the province of those who mediated with the gods – and goddesses – on behalf of the people. The ancients revered their sacred landscapes and, even if culture and civilization have moved on, that reverence remains imprinted in the land for those who come to rediscover it. To me, a sacred landscape provides a sense of coming home. No matter what the spiritual impulse behind such places – and there are many throughout the world –

Protected by Sarcen-stones, a Bluestone "needle" beside the Greensand Garnet-studded altar stone at Stonehenge echoes the Preseli Hills from which the Bluestones and the site's builders came. By planting these stones into the chalk, the ancients created a powerful energy-source, a geological "battery".

a sacred landscape takes me into the centre of myself. When I travel I carry a small piece of Flint with me, because it holds the essence of my home land – a valley that meanders among a vast, complex and exceedingly ancient sacred landscape studded with Flint. The further I delved into my local landscape, the more ancient I found it to be – and the more geo-energetic.

Landscape, mind and physiology

Research has shown that the geology and geophysics of our landscape influence us deeply, in the same way that the moon controls not just the tides of the planet's oceans, but also the tides of fluid within our bodies. It is much easier to enter an altered state of consciousness, or trance state, at some places than at others. Our physiological and psychological functioning is fundamentally affected by mineral ore, geomagnetism, geochemistry, volcanic activity and subsurface water and by the giant electrical conducting system beneath our feet: rock.

Within that system there are power nodes and Earth chakras. To our ancestors those nodes were awe-inspiring and sacred; they were *numinous* – filled with the mysterious power of the divine

– and sacred sites were built on them. Deeply attuned to each nuance of the landscape and its underlying geology, our ancient ancestors knew how to harness and manipulate natural forces in the landscape to affect behaviour and achieve altered states.

Scientists today are discovering geological bases to mind and mood alteration. Geochemical trace elements – such as copper, petrochemicals, zinc and lithium – in the rocks play a part; as may the movement of tectonic plates. Uneasy shifts in tectonic plates creates "transient, bizarre and unusual behaviours" and many of the world's sacred sites are placed at tectonic-plate junctions or on the joining point of two distinct geologies, creating a "liminal space", a portal between worlds.

Some ancient sites were created using stones from the site itself, but, all over the world, ancient people also moved stones from one location to another to energetically connect the two and to enhance the energy of the native rocks, or of the landscape. Almost all of the additional stones were Quartz-rich rocks that amplified the electromagnetic energy at a site. You can continue the tradition.

Spirits of place

In contrast to the lost souls trapped at a site (see page 122), spirits of place are guardian beings that may or may not have been human at one time. Often they were priests or priestesses,

Purpurite, Rose Quartz and Halite all assist the Earth to heal.

or geomancers, who once lived and worked at the site and who elected to stay on as guardians. These guardians know the site and its energetic functioning intimately. Enlisting the assistance of spirits of place can make a great difference to the effectiveness of your healing work at a sacred site. Always ask their permission before entering the site and spend a few moments communing with them to ascertain what is needed. Some guardian spirits appreciate an offering. For example, at the Pipestone quarry in Minnesota, USA, the Nations obtain Catlinite for their pipes and other sacred objects. But, before quarrying begins, they offer tobacco to five guardian boulders. In her temple at Karnak in Egypt, My Lady Sekhmet much prefers beer!

Sacred sites and Earth healing

Sacred sites lie on power nodes – the focal points for energy lines radiating out over vast distances. Many sites are located on the Earth's major or minor chakras (see pages 69–72). For these reasons, layouts at the sites themselves, or placed on a map over their locations, are excellent ways to heal and restore the energy of a whole area and the Earth's matrix grid (see pages 66–8).

SUITABLE STONES FOR RESTORING ENERGY AT SACRED SITES

The following is a list of stones that are particularly useful for restoring energy at sacred sites. Use one or a combination of these, or any revered stone from near the site itself.

Aragonite (lilac, blue, white and brown), Aswan Granite, Black Tourmaline, Brandenberg Amethyst, Clear Quartz, Eye of the Storm (Judy's Jasper), Fire and Ice (Rainbow Quartz), Flint, Golden Healer Quartz, Graphic Smoky Quartz, Grey Granite from the local area, Halite, Pink Granite, Preseli Bluestone with chalk, Purpurite, Menalite, Rhodozite, Rose Quartz, Selenite, Shiva Lingam, Smoky Elestial Quartz, Smoky Quartz, Spirit Quartz, Tangerine Dream or other Lemurians, Trigonic Quartz

GETTING TO KNOW YOUR LOCAL SACRED SITE

Crystals: whatever feels appropriate for your locality

1   Tending local sites contributes to the energetic health of the whole landscape. If you don't already know, ascertain where your nearest local sacred site is. This may not be obvious, particularly if it has fallen out of use. Natural features such as caves, groves of trees, rocky outcrops, pools and any places that make your feet tingle and your hair stand on end are all possibilities. Or, you may find structures built on ancient mounds or the foundations of much older temples. A "notch" on the horizon, an alignment of stones, or even a hole in a rock through which you can observe the sunrise or sunset at the solstices or equinoxes points to ancient use. There are also modern sites, such as the memorials at the site of the Twin Towers or at Hiroshima. Even in a city you can find sacred space. Choose a site and make it your own.

2   Once you have found your site, tend it energetically. Spend time there. Meditate in it. Ascertain whether its guardian is still in residence. Take your chosen crystals for a "getting to know you" session and lay out a Sunburst grid (see page 51) there to activate the site's energies. Go back to the site as often as you can, but also aim to connect energetically from wherever you are, simply by thinking about the site and holding a crystal associated with it.

Flint is found at many sacred places in the world. It stabilizes the energies and forms a portal to other worlds.

THE EARTH DEVAS

The Earth has many beings that may be glimpsed with the psychic inner eye. These beings have an energetic body rather than a physical one. They include the devas, spiritual forces or nature spirits, who are intimately connected to the state of the planet and assist its ecological balance. For some, the most important of these devas is Mother Earth. If you get into the habit of talking to the devas they guide you to where Earth healing is most needed and show you how it can be most effective.

Understanding the devas

The word deva means "shining one" in Sanskrit. There is said to be a "hierarchy" of devas that encompasses everything from the deva who looks after your local landscape, a wood, a mountain or a pond, to an elemental or crystal deva. The planetary deva has overall responsibility for the Earth. Famously, it was the ability of Theosophist and metaphysician Dorothy Maclean (born 1920) to communicate with devas – with the intelligence of nature – that led her, along with Peter and Eileen Caddy, to found the Findhorn community in 1962. In her book *To Hear the Angels Sing*, Maclean wrote of her encounter with a mountain deva that described itself as "of the Earth itself" and as existing "before and after man". The deva told Maclean that its consciousness was profoundly associated with that of the Earth and that the devas were the "great maintainers" of the planet, which functions as a living, breathing creature. However much humans change nature, they can never affect the devas, who persist for ever.

Mother Earth

To some people Mother Earth is the planetary deva, the head honcho of a hierarchy, rather like the head girl in a school. I prefer to think of her as Gaia, a living, breathing spirit who is divine and yet has taken on the nature of Earth. To me, she is female because that's how I've always seen her when we meet, but to the ancient Egyptians "she" was Geb, the Earth god. You can make up your own mind about how you view her – you'll have the opportunity to meet in the journey exercise on pages 88–9.

Crystal devas and oversouls

Crystals of a specific type share an overall consciousness, which could be called a deva, but I prefer "oversoul", a term coined by a UK crystal expert, Michael Eastwood, as it encompasses dimensions other than the Earth. Talking to the crystal oversoul helps you to cooperate together, expressed through your work with an individual crystal from that particular crystal family. Many oversouls have told me how pleased they are to be able to work in harmony with humans to heal the Earth through the individual expression of their energy. They feel that this is their function and it is why parts of the overall consciousness agreed to be torn from their roots deep in the earth – and why some crystals work their way to the surface to willingly offer themselves for this work.

Elemental devas

Elemental devas are connected to the elements of earth, air, fire, water and ether. Often used in magical workings, they may appear when you undertake elemental healing (see pages 104–5). If you explain your intention, they willingly cooperate with you.

Earth devas

Earth devas (of the non-elemental kind) act like guardian spirits and may manifest as spirits of place. These devas look after specific spots on Earth. For example, forests have their own special devas, as do the mountains. Waterfalls always have a deva or two in their rainbow spray. Earth devas may show themselves to you as bright lights flitting around a site, or as a gentle touch as you pass through.

COMMUNICATING WITH THE DEVAS

Devas communicate through telepathy or gentle nudges. They will send signals from nature – sudden sounds, rushes of wind or ripples in water. If you are not in harmony with nature, or if you disrespect it, or if your ego is in control, you are unlikely to be able to communicate with the devas. But if you sincerely and humbly offer to assist them as they maintain the Earth, they make their presence known. Watch for subtle mental pictures, gentle scents, soft touches or orbs of light. Meditate quietly with your eyes half closed and your other senses open to make a connection. You can then intuitively converse or dowse to discover exactly what the devas are asking you to do. Notice any impulses you may have and where your feet want to take you when visiting a site. The body often picks up the signals before the mind if we are alert to them.

The deva of Rose Quartz painted by the author on an Earth-healing workshop.

FERTILIZING THE HEART OF GAIA

This journey takes you into the body of Gaia herself, to take the light of the sun (or the moon) to revitalize and fertilize her very being. If you do not have a Fire and Ice crystal, you can use any Quartz with inclusions, or gaze at the photograph until you can close your eyes and still see it clearly. A Menalite helps you journey to the womb of Mother Earth. Avoid trying to make the journey while reading these instructions. Record them, leaving appropriate spaces, or ask a friend to read them to you, or read them through several times until you know them by heart.

FIRE-AND-ICE JOURNEY

Crystals: Fire and Ice, or included Quartz, or Menalite

Put your stone in the sun for an hour or two to collect the sun's energy (Menalite prefers moonlight). When the crystal is fully charged and ready to go, sit in a quiet space where you will not be disturbed and withdraw your attention from the outside world.

1   Holding the stone, sit quietly with your eyes closed and hold the intention that it lifts you up and transports you to the high Andes mountains – the stone knows where to go. You feel yourself rapidly travelling to a plateau surrounded by huge peaks. As you land the Earth devas come to greet you. They make this journey with you.

2   In front of you, you see a path leading down into a cave mouth. Follow the path until you enter the cave (the home of Gaia). Hold your crystal high – its light guides you.

3   The path is broad and wide and it winds down and down into the heart of the mountain passing many crystals on the way. You can hear the crystal oversouls and the Earth devas

speaking to you, lending their support to you and thanking you for helping the Earth in this way.

4   Eventually you come to an immense cave. In the centre of the cave is a huge Rhodochrosite stone heart. This is the heart of Gaia that beats very slowly, once every 100 years or so. Allow yourself to feel the presence of the spirit of Mother Earth and feel the love that she has for you.

5   Place your crystal on the heart of Mother Earth to fertilize her with the light of the sun. (Or place Menalite in her womb, the cave.) Hold the intention that the light will heal the Earth and its energy grid and support life on the planet.

6   When you are ready, make your way back up the path and out onto the plateau. The Earth devas accompany you.

7   Hold the intention to return to where your body waits. Take a few deep breaths, wriggle your fingers and toes, stand up and stretch. Stamp your feet to ground yourself.

Making this journey work for you

If you have a local site sacred to the Earth Mother, the Virgin Mary or a female deity, you could make the journey to that site either in your imagination or in actuality. Place the sun-charged crystal at the heart centre of the site and let it radiate its energy outward.

Fire and Ice Quartz. If this is not available, use a Quartz with plenty of inclusions.

SEEDING THE EARTH

In India, 12 great Shiva Lingams, or *jyotirlingas*, are set up to represent the seed energies of the universe and unite the dualities (male–female, god–goddess), forming a cosmic union. Crystals elsewhere have been used on the Earth like acupuncture needles, to restore balance to the land. They may be placed upright, laid out flat, or buried in the earth for a long-term grid. Dowse for their position and hold the intention that they harmonize an existing grid, bringing it in line with others in the area.

Needles of stone

Across the world needles of stone stand tall. Some are natural, others have been carefully shaped from columns of rock, and many have been transported great distances to be set up as an altar or standing stone. These keep the Earth's energy grid anchored in place and recharge it with the energies of the luminaries (the sun or moon) or the deities. In many ancient cultures, the luminaries and the deities were one and the same.

A Shiva Lingam represents the ascending energy of consciousness and the creative force in nature, reflecting the mountain, the thunder cloud or the tree. A Lingam sits in a receptive *yoni* basin to symbolize the union of masculine and feminine forces, and the creation and dissolution cycle in the universe. According to the *Skanda Purana*, an ancient Hindu scripture, the Lingam represents the all-pervading space in which the whole universe is in a process of constant creation and dissolution. By its subtle movement, a swinging Lingam can create a *yoni*, in exactly the same way as a small movement around a fixed point describes a circle. This movement reflects the great cosmic circles – the apparent movement of the stars, planets and nebulae across the sky – as well as natural phenomena in nature. The planets circle as they revolve around the sun, the Lingam of our solar system, which moves around its central principle or axis, the galactic centre. But in turn, the sun itself is revolving around other stars and creating a *yoni* or circle of its own.

It has been suggested that ancient peoples set up Stonehenge in England to unite male and female and represent the cosmic cycles. It certainly has sun-aligned central stones, but it also once had an outer ring of Bluestones that were aligned to the long cycle of the lunar eclipse. The Bluestones themselves were set within an enclosing bank, which could represent the womb of Mother

In ancient temples, needles of stone brought the energy of the sun to the earth to fertilize it. This one is at Karnak temple complex at Luxor in Egypt.

Earth. This uniting of masculine and feminine creates a kundalini (creative) force. Together the male and female energies form a spiral that weaves around itself up the human spine, and also powers the Earth. Both forces are necessary to create this dynamic motion. The Earth's main line of kundalini has recently been said to have moved from the mountains of the Himalaya, where it had been located for many years, to the Rocky Mountains in North America and the Andes in South America. Much Earth healing work has been needed to bed this force into its new home and it is still settling in. Setting up a Shiva Lingam or placing a needle of stone into the earth on an energy point can assist this settling and power a new vibration.

It is said that everyone has their own Lingam within the earth into which the signature of their soul has been alchemically embedded during the years of the Lingam's creation in the body of Mother Earth. It acts as a kind of Akashic Record – a subtle, etheric recorder – for the soul's journey. The Lingam draws out our soul qualities, but it also passes them into the earth to assist with Earth healing and the activation of the new kundalini line.

SETTING UP A SHIVA LINGAM

You can set up any tall pillar-like stone, large crystal point or obelisk to harmonize masculine and feminine energies in your environment. When you have chosen your stone – either by dowsing or intuiting which to use – select a site where your Lingam will not be disturbed. Bed the flat or rounded end of your Lingam into a ring or bowl that acts as the receiving yoni. I use a metal ring for this purpose and pad it with a cloth to avoid scratches. When you have set up your Lingam, visualize it harmonizing "above" and "below", and radiating its power into the ground beneath it.

DETOXIFYING THE PLANET

Pollution may be chemical (such as heavy metals) or energetic (such as noise, heat, excessive light or even negative thought patterns). Laying out a crystal grid intended to detoxify heals the damage from pollution and encourages the land to renew itself.

Pollution then and now

Pollution is not something new: the Earth has been subject to toxic influence for millennia. Volcanoes have always belched out noxious fumes, and some ancient manufacturing processes such as metal working were just as polluting as modern ones – albeit on a smaller scale. Core ice samples taken from glaciers in Greenland contain greenhouse gases associated with 2,000-year-old Greek, Roman and Chinese metal production. Leather tanning, carried out more than 9,000 years ago, also left toxic residues in the soil and water. Large-scale agriculture produced methane gases. Usually thought to be linked to post-industrial activities, levels of particulates (microscopic particles that irritate the lungs) almost equal to those of the modern day have been found in the lungs of ancient Egyptian mummies. For a long time nature could deal with the problems. Now, though, pollution is too widespread for nature to manage, affecting the land, sea and air.

There is also the problem of the energetic pollution that results from hatred. You know that you can help to counter the effects of physical pollution by using fewer chemicals, recycling and so on, but you can also do a great deal about energetic contamination. Guard your thoughts. Do not indulge in toxic thinking – keep a crystal in your pocket to remind you to focus on the positive. Then, create crystal layouts to soak up the energetic pollution in your world and transform the thinking that created it in the first place. Begin with the layout on the following page.

DETOXIFYING LAYOUT

Layout: Complex Star of David

Crystals: Black Tourmaline, Halite or Malachite;
Graphic Smoky Quartz or Smoky Quartz; Eye of
the Storm or Selenite; Rhodozite

You can place this layout anywhere there is pollution. Lay it onto
the ground, or on a map or photograph of the area you want to
heal. (You can even lay it around a person to help him or her
with a detox.) Halite is an all-purpose cleanser and Malachite is
particularly suitable for radiation or emotional toxicity. You will
need three sets of one type of crystal (each set containing six
crystals). Cleanse the crystals before you begin (see pages 19–21).

1   Hold your first set of cleansed crystals in your hands
    and dedicate them to detoxifying the land.
2   Lay them in a star with a crystal at each point (see page 45).
    Complete the circuit with a wand.
3   Dedicate the next set and use it to create a star offset
    from the first. Complete that star's circuit with a wand.
4   Dedicate the final set and use it to create a third star
    between the first two. Complete that circuit with a wand.
5   Use the power of your mind to see the star "fire up" –
    it radiates its detoxifying energies outward into the land,
    absorbing the energetic pollution and transmuting it.
6   Place a large Graphic Smoky Quartz or Smoky Quartz
    at the bottom of the layout to anchor it (see page 96).
7   Place an Eye of the Storm or Selenite in the centre, and
    a ring of Rhodozite around the whole layout to encourage
    regeneration.
8   Leave the layout in place for as long as possible, cleansing
    it regularly. You may need to add other crystals or stars to
    the layout as the days progress, so listen to your intuition.

BASIC EARTH CLEARING AND RECHARGING

Laying your crystals directly on the ground – whether it is pebbly, grassy, sandy, rocky, forest, barren or fertile – is a great way to inject healing energies into the Earth and to harness the power of the sun and the moon to purify, fertilize and stimulate new growth and abundance. Direct placement is particularly effective if the site has sacred connotations.

Choosing a layout; seeking the stones

Any one of the crystal layouts in this book is suitable for laying on the ground to clear and recharge the earth. Dowse (see pages 22–3) or use your intuition to select the right one for you. If you are placing the stones at a sacred site, the site's spirit guardian will help you with your choice. If you intuitively feel that a different layout from those in the book would be best, go for it!

Carefully dowse or ask for the highest possible guidance as to which crystals are suitable for your particular layout. Remember that the most appropriate crystals to use will change with each layout *and the person placing them*. Ensure that you have cleansed your own energies and that they are at their optimum before you begin this work. Bring only positive energy to this task; keep your thoughts and emotions calm. Take care to avoid making negative statements or idle chatter, or having toxic thoughts near a layout, which will pick up and amplify the negativity. Remain positive.

Finally, check and cleanse your crystals carefully each time you lay them. Putting extraneous or "unclean" crystals into a layout can not only throw the layout off balance, but also introduce inappropriate or contaminated energies and negate the intended effect of the layout.

The Stonehenge heelstone anchor – note the grumpy face (simulacra) in the rock. The road behind the stone cuts the energy flow of the circle, which requires constant reconnection. Of course, the road would not have been there when the circle was built.

Anchoring your layout

In the same way that a heel stone anchors the energy of a stone circle into the landscape, a layout benefits from having an anchoring stone placed at some distance from it. Typical anchoring stones are Granite, Flint, Quartz-rich rock or Milk (Opaque White) Quartz. You can also use large Smoky Quartz or Smoky Quartz Elestials for this task.

OUTDOOR LAYOUTS

- Activate your palm chakras (see pages 24–5) and the dantien (see page 29) before you begin.
- Cleanse your stones and state your intention.
- Dowse or use your intuition to select the spot for your outdoor layout.
- Lay the grid out roughly to begin with, then use a pole on the ground or a ruler on a photograph (allow for camera distortion) to establish that radiating lines are straight. Adjust the stones if necessary.
- Join the lines of the grid, if appropriate.

2013 SUMMER SOLSTICE AND "SUPER MOON" LAYOUTS

Layout: Sunburst variant (see page 51)

Crystals: Shiva Lingam, Smoky Elestial Quartz, Flint, Lemurian, Citrine, Selenite, Granite, Chalk

Practical application: recharging the landscape

As the 2013 summer solstice was closely followed by a "super moon" when the moon was at its nearest to Earth and its energy particularly potent, I wanted to use the energies generated to recharge my local sacred landscape. The first alignment faced the midsummer pre-solstice sunset and was placed on one of 12 radiating sun-lines at Knowlton Henge. Knowlton is a chalk ditch and bank henge, perfect for creating an energetic battery for Earth healing. The intention was to charge up the stones with the energy of the sun and transfer it to a new solstice sunrise layout the next morning to fertilize the surrounding area.

The layout at Knowlton Henge. The anchor stone for this grid was a large piece of ironstone in the ruined church behind it.

I walked around the henge to feel where the layout wanted to be placed. My feet tingled strongly as I reached the westerly line toward the dying sun. I laid out a straight line first. The Shiva Lingam focal point of the layout would become the centre of a solstice sunrise layout the next day. The energies passed through a large Smoky Elestial to purify them and a Citrine ball to revitalize them, before being stored in the Lingam. The Elestial Smoky Quartz also acted as a purifier for the grid, its cleansing effect on the earth energies of the henge passing out through Lemurian Quartzes radiating out from the central alignment.

Having refertilized the area through a Shiva Lingam-based sunrise layout the next day, I wanted to channel the energy of the "super moon" to initiate further regeneration. The layout could not be made at Knowlton as it was crowded with people celebrating this extraordinary moon. So, the layout was placed in my garden, which is bedded on a thick layer of chalk. It is on a leyline linking Knowlton and the termination of the Dorset Cursus, the longest and oldest ritual way in England, and so would radiate power throughout the energetic network. In front of a Buddha statue,

A Shiva Lingam formed the focus for the pre-solstice sunset and solstice sunrise layouts.

The "super moon" grid laid out in the author's garden, ready for adjustment.

it would bathe in the light of the huge full moon. Large Smoky Quartz points, Smoky Elestials and local blue and yellow Flints drew in and cleansed negative energies. At the centre, a Selenite moon tower brought pure light into the layout, which was radiated out through large Quartz points. The Smoky Quartz pointed inward to draw in energy; the Clear Quartz pointed outward to channel the energy out again. A Preseli Bluestone "dragon's head" behind the Buddha anchored the grid and connected it to the Stonehenge network, a few miles away.

Making the layout work for you

You can use the same procedure for placing any layout straight onto the earth. If appropriate, dowse for the exact alignment and position of the crystals but, as you develop your crystal intuition more strongly, you will instinctively know where to place the crystals and recognize when a layout is aligned and fully active.

EARTH HEALING ON THE MAP

Placing crystals on a map or a photograph in a geometric pattern transfers the crystal energy to the actual geographical area through the process of entrainment. The layout does not have to be large to be effective and you can leave it in place. Alternatively, you can use an Earth-healing mandala (sacred geometric diagram) to transfer healing to the whole Earth.

Laying crystals in two dimensions

Mandalas are multi-dimensional and create great energy, but laying crystals on a map or picture of the Earth to create your own sacred geometry is just as effective. Your pattern weaves a multi-layered grid around the Earth to channel healing to wherever the Earth needs it. Dowse to ascertain which layout is appropriate (see pages 22–3) or create your own mandala. Place appropriate crystals on each of the points to ground higher dimensional energy and to bring balance to the Earth. As you lay out your crystals on the mandala, photograph or map, consciously feel that you are part of the whole, part of the living entity that is our Earth. You are one of her children. Feel your cosmic connection, too, so that you draw in universal energy to enhance the healing process. Hold the intention that the crystals will heal and support the Earth. As you place each crystal, feel the energy tingle in your palm chakras. Transfer this energy to the map as you let go of the crystal. Perhaps say a prayer or an affirmation as you do so.

Practical application: healing towers

A visionary Earth-healing mandala (see page 158) inspired one of my workshops to create an Anandalite™ layout centred around a spirit-type Anandalite™ that looked like two towers. We put Blue Flash Anandalite™ on the points of the mandala and surrounded the crystal in the centre with Rose Quartz hearts and Rhodozite. Created just after the death of Osama Bin Laden, the layout was intended to release from the Twin Towers site, and elsewhere, all the grief and misery Bin Laden had caused, and replace it with peace, forgiveness and healing. We envisaged this sense of peace radiating right across the USA and the globe. This layout was itself part of an on-going process of dismantling old structures to make way for a new level of understanding.

Some of the crystals used to create
the Twin Towers healing layout.

CREATING HARMONY

A lemiscate layout pulls cosmic, high-vibrational energy downward to meet Earth's own energy. It transmutes this earth energy and infuses it with a new frequency that cleanses and purifies. Use the layout for either small areas or the whole globe via a map. Remember to cleanse your crystals (see pages 19–21) and activate your dantien (see page 29) before you begin.

EARTH-HARMONY LAYOUT

Layout: Lemiscate (see page 48)

Crystals: Selenite and Brown Aragonite, or any combination of high- and earthy-vibration crystals; Elestial Quartz or Smoky Brandenberg; Rhodozite

1   Hold your high-vibration crystals in your hands and state your intention to bring in high-frequency cosmic energies to help the Earth (or a specific place).
2   Lay the crystals, beginning at the central point up the left-hand side, around the top and down to right.
3   Place an Elestial Quartz or Smoky Brandenberg at the central, crossover point to ground the energy.
4   Hold your earthy-vibration stones and state your intention to bring earth energies up to the Earth (or a specific place).
5   Lay these crystals beginning at the centre, moving down the right-hand side to the bottom and up the left-hand side back to the centre, to complete the lemiscate. Join the whole circuit with the power of your mind or a crystal wand.
6   Wait for a few moments before placing a ring of Rhodozite around the lemiscate to anchor it.
7   Leave in place for as long as possible, paying attention to the layout at least once a day and renewing your intention.

This Leminiscate, using Selenite, Malachite, Halite and Rhodozite, was laid out to calm and detoxify energies following the Japanese earthquake in 2011 that damaged nuclear power stations and spilled radioactivity into the Pacific.

ELEMENTAL HEALING

The ancients believed that the world was composed of five building blocks or elements, each reflecting various states of matter: earth (the solid state), air (gaseous), fire (plasmic), water (liquid) and ether (the quintessential animating and unifying principle, the space in which the elements exist).

Balancing the elements

The Babylonian epic of creation, the Enuma Elish, tells us that the world was founded upon five cosmic elements: sea, earth, fire, wind and sky. This is perhaps the earliest known reference to five elements, although they provide the foundation of many other systems, too. Over time, some systems dropped the fifth aspect; others have different elemental combinations. In astrology, earth represents the body; air, the mind; water, the emotions; and fire, the intuitive and initiatory process of creation. It is through the transmutation of the elements that alchemy takes place.

Although there is a consensus throughout the world that there are elements, various parts of the world view the elements disparately. In Traditional Chinese Medicine, Feng Shui and Ayurveda the elements control each other in an enduring cycle. In Feng Shui (and other systems) they also relate to the cardinal directions (north, south, east and west). As with the chakras, the elements may be associated with particular colours: earth is brown or green; air, yellow or grey; fire, red or orange; water, blue; and ether, white. (You do not need to use these colours for your crystal choices, though.)

Depending upon where you live, and as elemental systems often grew out of local conditions, one system may feel more suited to you than another. You can work with the basic elements without needing to know your local system, but common sense may tell you in which element you reside. In an exceedingly hot place, you are under the dominion of fire. An exceedingly wet place puts you into water's influence; and windy is, of course, air. Cold could well indicate the solid state of matter, earth – but, then, so could a fertile area or a forest. Wet and windy climates are under the influence of water and wind; hot and dry ones, of fire and air. You can use crystals attuned to the elements to compensate for missing elements or to harmonize all the elements. For example, if an area is prone to flooding, balancing it out with the drying action of earth or air crystals could be helpful. Similarly, earth-type crystals could bring energetic abundance and creativity to a barren, dry or fiery landscape.

ELEMENT-BALANCING LAYOUT

Layout: Pentangle (see page 46)

Crystals: See below

To create elemental harmony, arrange this layout over a map of your local area or of the world. Use my suggestions, or dowse or pay attention to your intuition and local knowledge to select your crystals. Place the crystals in the order shown and remember to go back to the first point to join up the circuit. Cleanse your crystals (see pages 19–21) and activate your dantien (see page 29) before you begin.

1   Top point (Ether). *Suggested crystals*: Anandalite™, Brandenberg, Shiva Lingam, Tektites, Spirit Quartz
2   Bottom right (Earth). *Suggested crystals*: Black Tourmaline, Eye of the Storm, Flint, Menalite, Rhodozite
3   Top left (Air). *Suggested crystals*: Fire and Ice, Herkimer Diamond, Preseli Bluestone, Selenite
4   Top right (Fire). *Suggested crystals*: Bumble Bee Jasper, Granite, Rose Quartz, Tangerine Dream Lemurians
5   Bottom left (Water). *Suggested crystals*: Blue Aragonite, Halite, Stromatolite, Trigonic Quartz

ENVIRONMENTAL ENHANCEMENT

Crystals imbue your environment with beneficial energies and can help you to reverse environmental degradation, restoring the vitality of the land. Ideally, to harness these energies you will create a layout using Tangerine Dream Lemurians. However, you need to have had some practice in handling crystal energies before you use this exceedingly powerful crystal. You can use Tangerine, Golden or Apricot Quartz instead.

Revitalizing an area: Tangerine Dreams

Tangerine Dream Lemurians are absolutely amazing crystals. Working with them took me to an extremely high vibration where it was possible to get an overview of the evolution of the Earth – and humanity – and to recognize my role within that.

Lemurians remind us to do our own work and attend to our own evolution. They also facilitate the evolution of others and the Earth, so it is important to tend your own energies before working with this layout. Otherwise, others could sap your energy or you may tarnish theirs. Showing us that we are multi-dimensional beings, these crystals pierce the illusion of separateness in physical incarnation and remind us that the journey of healing is of re-membering (bringing back together) our spiritual selves. Lemurians also teach us that time is an illusion of physical incarnation. They show us how to move beyond its boundaries into the true reality of unity consciousness. When placed in a layout, they revitalize all the elements and the Earth's grid over a vast distance.

REVITALIZING LAYOUT

Layout: Sunburst (see page 51)

Crystals: Smoky Quartz or Elestial Smoky Quartz;
Tangerine Dream Lemurians (or Tangerine, Golden or
Apricot Quartz); additional Lemurians or clear Quartz
points; Rhodozite

I first made this layout using 72 Tangerine Dream Lemurians
arranged round a Stellar Beam Calcite, but using even a single
Tangerine Dream adds potent energy. I also incorporated Clear,
Smoky, Citrine, Pink and Chlorite Lemurians, plus Golden Healers
into the rays of my first layout, but you can substitute Quartz
points, especially if you are a new to crystal work. Cleanse your
crystals (see pages 19–21) and activate your dantien (see page 29)
before you begin. Use a map or lay the grid directly on the ground.

1   Place a large, dedicated Smoky Quartz or Elestial Smoky
    Quartz over the centre of the area you wish to revitalize.
    This will draw off and purify negative energies.
2   Hold the remaining crystals in your hands. State your
    intention to revitalize the land.
3   Lay the Tangerine Dream Lemurians around the central
    crystal in a sunburst; or place a single stone facing south.
4   Continue laying Lemurians (or Quartz points), lengthening
    each line in turn until it intuitively feels – or dowsing tells
    you – it is the right length (lines do not have to be equal).
5   After a few minutes add Rhodozite to the end of each line
    to stabilize and ground the energies.
6   Visualize the layout lighting up, pouring out energy into the
    surrounding land. Leave the layout in place until you feel it
    has done its work. Then, deconstruct it carefully, removing
    each line in the order you placed it. Leave the energetic
    imprint to go on energizing the land, if appropriate.

BRINGING IN MORE LOVE

Everywhere and everyone benefits from having more love.
A multi-armed spiral layout draws in unconditional, universal love and radiates it out to the surrounding area in an endless flow of peace and tranquillity. Place one such layout at the centre of your home to draw in love and radiate it out to your community.

Unconditional love

Crystals teach us that unconditional love means opening your heart to a flow of universal energy. It does not judge or make conditions; it simply is. Nor does it mean that you have to become a victim to love. Rather, it means that you do not need to put up with what so often masquerades under the guise of love. You don't have to be manipulated, misused, abused or taken advantage of while saying "It's alright, I still love you." You can set boundaries.

Crystals show us that to do anything other than to love unconditionally is to disable another person, holding them in detrimental patterns that stop their growth. Instead, standing in your own quiet crystal space, you remain unaffected by what someone else does, abstaining from judgement. You see someone's potential, but you don't force that person to change. You don't pretend that someone is "perfect" when their behaviour is not, but you still love them, accepting them as they are. When you love others unconditionally, you accept their humanity, while also honouring your own. When you do this, detrimental situations fall away and you invite more love into your life. This applies to groups of people as much as to a single person.

If you need love you don't have to demand it from someone else, or suck them dry. Reach for a crystal instead. You can find love deep within yourself and at the heart of the universe. Crystals take you into an enveloping sense of abiding, unconditional love and acceptance. Wrapped in their nurturing energy, you are love.

LOVE-ENHANCING LAYOUT

Layout: Multi-armed Spiral

Crystals: Rose Quartz, Rhodochrosite

Create this layout in a place where you can see it often. Cleanse your stones (see pages 19–21) and activate your dantien (see page 29) before you begin.

1   Hold your crystals in your hands, open your palm chakras and state your intention to receive and radiate love. Feel how the crystals instantly emit powerful waves of love in response. Allow your heart to fill with unconditional love.
2   Take the crystals to your heart for a few moments to make a connection of love.
3   Place a large Rose Quartz in the centre of the spiral.
4   Next, lay small Rhodochrosite and Rose Quartz tumble stones or hearts along the spiral arms.
5   Place your hand on your heart, sit quietly and contemplate the layout through half-closed eyes.
6   When the love in your heart begins to overflow, let it go out to all those around you. Refill your heart as you do so, so that there is a constant infilling and out-flowing of love. You are love incarnate and embodied. Let the love flow into the earth.
7   Leave the layout in position for as long as possible.

OXYGEN REPLENISHMENT

Oxygen in our atmosphere is the reason that life as we know it flourishes. But as more forests – the lungs of Mother Earth – are cut down, and pollution is pumped into the air, the planet struggles to maintain its biosphere. Crystals can provide energetic support for the cocoon of life-giving oxygen around us.

The breath of life

Without oxygen many life forms on Earth would die. Even deep within the Earth's crust, in pockets of sedimentary rocks, there are oxygen-producing bacterial lifeforms. Stromatolites are three-billion-year-old fossils created by blue-green cyanobacteria that flourished in the primeval soup. They were partially responsible for the creation of Earth's atmosphere. Through photosynthesis, they absorbed carbon dioxide and excreted oxygen, making them a perfect choice for supporting Earth's atmosphere now. Kambaba Jasper (Green Stromatolite) and Stromatolite hold an ancient, and wise, earth energy. They harmonize you with the cycles of the natural world, attuning your personal biorhythm to that of the planet. Stromatolite is beneficial for the lungs – of the human body and of the planet. Meditate with it to hear nature's wisdom and find a mentor for your spiritual path.

DEEP BREATHING

To rapidly improve your own oxygen intake, and that of the planet, hold a Stromatolite just below your navel and *breathe*. Stand with your legs slightly bent, making sure you feel balanced. Take a long, slow breath right down to the stone and feel your breath meet the energy of the Stromatolite. As you slowly breathe out, push the synergized life-giving energy down into the earth below you. Repeat five times without pausing.

BREATH-OF-LIFE LAYOUT

Layout: Inverted Pentangle (see page 46)

Crystals: Stromatolite or Kambaba Jasper

For this layout you need a map or a picture of the Amazon rainforest, or any area where trees are being cut down or where oxygen is depleted. You can also use this layout to restore the oxygen balance in a polluted atmosphere. If you prefer or if it's appropriate, you can place this layout on the ground and leave it undisturbed. Cleanse your crystals (see pages 19–21) and activate your dantien (see page 29) before you begin.

1   Hold your cleansed crystals in your hands for a few moments and open your palm chakras. Feel the energy of the stones passing up your arms and down into your lungs. State your intention to support the lungs of the planet.

2   Place your first stone at the bottom of the layout – remembering to place the pentangle upside down (this grounds the energy).

3   Place successive crystals on the points of the pentangle, then place crystals at the points of intersection.

4   When the layout is complete, join up the points using your mind or a crystal wand to complete the circuit and to focus the energy deep into the lungs of the planet.

5   Breathe rhythmically and slowly for a few moments in tune with the planet.

6   Leave the layout for as long as possible to support the planet.

Stromatolite

IMPROVING
WATER QUALITY

Since ancient times, water has been regarded as inherently sacred. We are conceived from a fluid and float in a liquid matrix in the womb. Blood and lymph flow around our body. Birth is heralded by the breaking of the waters. As the Hungarian physiologist Albert Szent-Gyorgyi put it: "Water is life's mater and matrix, mother and medium. There is no life without water."

The waters of life

The flow of water around the globe helps to convey earth energies, but can also create blockages in the Earth's matrix grid. The more energetically pure the water, the better the energy flow.

Water can be sensitive to emanations and thoughts. It rapidly absorbs vibrations, which can in turn be used to heal it. Trigonic Quartz has a powerful link to the cosmic tides and to the Earth's poles and geo-currents. Its energy flows through the body in waves and is experienced at different temperatures according to your body type – and the same is true for the Earth and its geology. Simply placing a Trigonic in a metal bowl filled with water and tapping the bowl transfers the crystal's vibrations to the water.

Making a Trigonic essence

Place your Trigonic in a Tibetan or other metal bowl and cover it with natural springwater. Tap the edge of the bowl to instantly transfer the crystal's energy into the liquid, covering the surface of the water in triangles. Pour this energized fluid into the nearest river or sea to take the Trigonic's vibrations around the world. (To make a Quartz or other crystal Earth-healing essence, place the crystal in natural springwater in a glass bowl and leave it in the sun for several hours. Pour the infused water onto the ground or down a drain, from where it will eventually reach the oceans.)

This Trigonic Quartz has been placed in a glass bowl to show the required water level (Trigonic essences are usually made in a metal bowl).

Practical application: liquid gold

You may remember the oil spill in the Gulf of Mexico in 2010. That was my first introduction to working with Trigonic Quartz. The new Quartz expressed a wish to assist in healing the consequences of the spillage, so I took it to several workshops over the next few months. Each time it corresponded to a new phase of the rescue operation and its connection with the water on the planet became more profound. We asked everyone who had a Trigonic to dedicate their stone to healing this gash in the Earth and stemming the bleeding for the highest good of the planet.

During the first workshop we laid out a grid combining Trigonics with Herkimer Diamonds and sent our attention to the Gulf. We had had to change venue owing to an overpowering smell of oil from a (newly serviced) boiler. This followed my having had a problem with the fuel cap on my (diesel) car on the way to the workshop. These were signals from the universe that we needed to undertake the crystal work.

We began a layout and visualization to contain the oil spill. In my own visualization, the hole was plugged with a large Trigonic around which huge Herkimer Diamonds were inserted. Lightning and electricity flashed all around and turned spilled oil into

Herkimers (which, like oil, are carbon-based). The Herkimers went to all the places where the oil had spilled and transmuted it to a golden oil that would lubricate the Earth's matrix grid. Whales and dolphins brought healing water from a spot just off the coast of Brazil, where five major ocean currents meet; and Brandenbergs brought powerful earth energy from their source in Namibia. The Trigonics told me that we could, apparently, turn the flow back on itself – just as in martial arts when you can use an opponent's own energy to flip them over.

As I drove home there was an announcement that "heavy mud" was being used to plug the spill. But it wasn't enough. The Trigonics pointed out that this disaster had a great deal to do with our greed for oil. Mother Earth had shown us that we could not remain indifferent to the removal of one of her bodily fluids. This was a good moment to remind ourselves that ethically mined crystals, removed with due care and consideration for the environment, help to heal our planet and ourselves, but wholesale destruction to pull them out can only be disastrous.

I laid a grid on my dining room table. It was very powerful and best placed where it wouldn't be disturbed or disturb people (I initially slept over it and had to hastily relocate my bed as I was so wired I couldn't sleep). I used the Trigonics in conjunction with Fire and Ice, which had offered to help with re-energizing the Earth, plus Brandenbergs, Lemurians and Golden Herkimer Diamonds with Smoky Elestials to stabilize the grid. The whole was joined up and activated by a Tangerine Dream Lemurian point. The grid grew organically and soon had several other crystals including Himalayan Growth Interference and Nirvana Quartzes around it.

After each workshop, with serendipitous synchronicity, a new method of plugging and containment was announced. Step by step the spill was slowly coming under control. I felt that we – through the Trigonics – were participating in this process. This kind of "magical thinking" (see box, opposite) is not egotistical. Rather, it cooperates with the higher forces and the Earth devas to bring about a desired outcome.

The media said the oil was being captured, but the feeling from the Trigonics was that the cleaning up and transmutation process still needed assistance. For this reason, I added a Shift crystal. The next news bulletin said there had been a hurricane in the Gulf. It scattered the oil. All part of the process!

The grid continued to evolve and went to several more workshops before it simply drifted out of my awareness. I didn't reassemble it. I assumed it had done its work. The well had indeed been capped. Later, a report said that the consequences of the spill had been somewhat fewer than anticipated, because a new bacteria had "gobbled up the oil". I keep going back to that first picture of the Herkimers and Trigonics working together to transmute the oil. Did they energetically manufacture a bacterium in the process? Or was that tiny organism, like the Trigonics themselves, waiting to awaken in the Earth's time of need?

Making the layout work for you

If there is a body of polluted or stagnant water near to you, or a similar disaster occurs anywhere in the world, lay out a Herkimer and Quartz sunburst, points facing inward, around a Trigonic Quartz – you need only one. Hold the intention that the Trigonic energetically purifies the water and re-energizes it. You can also pour Trigonic essence into the site to strengthen the effect.

MAGICAL THINKING

In psychology, "magical thinking" is a negative concept: a misconception that your actions influence the world around you. In Earth healing it is positive: your thoughts and actions can indeed have an effect and you are able to use your thought processes for the greater good.

ANCHORING
THE EARTH

If you live in a volcanic or earthquake zone, such as that around the Mediterranean or the Pacific "Ring of Fire", you may experience the rumblings of Mother Earth on virtually a daily basis. You can mitigate the detrimental effects of this on your own energy field and that of the Earth by placing Aragonite around your home or on a map over the location of your home. Sometimes the earth simply has to release excessive tension through an earthquake or volcanic action. Hold the intention for the release to be in a region and in such a way that it does least harm.

Earth stabilizers

The brown "sputnick" form of Aragonite makes an excellent earth anchor. Bury it at each corner of your property or lay it into a stabilizing grid indoors, such as the Star of David (see page 45). Place the grid in- or outside where it will not be disturbed. You can also lay Aragonites on a map of the wider area. Use a Graphic Smoky Quartz at the base to anchor the energy. In fact, this stone is particularly useful as it was born out of enormous pressure itself. The layout does not have to be large to be energetically effective, as it transfers its energy through entrainment with the larger field.

BORROWING VIRTUE

Your crystals don't need to be massive to transmit their healing energy effectively. There is a simple technique that boosts the power of smaller crystals. Place them on a large version of the same crystal and hold the intention that the energies entrain to work together at their most powerful.

Practical application: restoring energy in New Zealand

A friend in Christchurch, New Zealand, was experiencing violent aftershocks following a massive earthquake (there are more than 15,000 earthquakes in New Zealand every year, but this had been the biggest of them all). Her beautiful, peaceful home atmosphere had been wrecked by the energetic shock, even though the house itself had withstood the Earth's dramatic rumblings. My friend's own energy was severely depleted, too. Then came a second big quake. As she reported, "The whole community has lost so much over the past year and the level of fear has been terrible. Before yesterday the whole city precinct was just a skeleton of bones of buildings; now it will be a ghost city. The aftershocks are continuing around Christchurch on a lesser scale, but the seismologists have warned us of the possibility of another big quake within the next 12 months so everyone remains nervous." The whole area needed calming and healing.

My friend left New Zealand and called in to see me when she arrived in England. Fortunately, I had just acquired two rather remarkable pieces of self-healed Quartz, These stones had "mountains" naturally etched into them. One was a smaller version of the other and we put them together so that the small one could "borrow virtue" (see box, opposite) and draw on the energy of the bigger crystal. Our intention was that the two stones would continue to communicate in this way even when one of them was on the other side of the world. This is her report of the effects of the borrowed virtue back in New Zealand:

"Yesterday I settled the crystal next to the running stream of alpine waters at the front of my house – this is the place I saw when you handed me the crystal. The immediate surrounds are darkened by a natural, dense canopy of graciously aged trees dressed by an undergrowth of softly entwined and interwoven foliage. Shafts of sunlight sparkle on the water. If you sit quietly and withdraw from the external environment, you can hear voices from past times. As soon as I placed the crystal on the

Calming the quakes. This crystal was placed in dense
undergrowth next to a stream.

floor of leaves it became incandescent and almost appeared to be
radiating a living energy. The camera hasn't captured what I saw
but you will be able to see beyond the imagery."

As you can see from the photograph above, the crystal glowed
and the energy improved rapidly. I put the other crystal – the one
that was still in England – away quietly to do its work. I took it out
the other day and my formerly white stone had become murky
and grey – a lesson to me to cleanse it more often. I quickly put
it out in a thunderstorm, dipped it in a sacred well and placed
it in the sun for a recharge.

Making the layout work for you

If you live in an area that has been through any kind of earth-
shock, a large Clear or Smoky Quartz will help you to calm and
restore the energies of the place, as well as your own. Dowse
or intuit the placement for the stone and leave it there as long
as possible. Alternatively, you can bury large Aragonite crystals
in the ground to stabilize the energy in your area.

TRAUMA CLEARING

Upheaval, battle, conflict, genocide, Earth events, major and even minor accidents, or a devastating personal experience can leave a detrimental energy imprint at a site. All events, thoughts and emotions, especially toxic or traumatic ones, leave an imprint where they occur. When other people, especially those who are sensitive to atmospheres, walk into this energy field, they are adversely affected by it but may not recognize the cause.

A land calling for healing

I remember driving down Glen Coe in Scotland 40 years ago. The weather had been amazingly warm for the time of year, but as we drove down the Great Glen a blizzard closed in. I thought my shivers, shudders and overwhelming nausea were the result of the sudden temperature change, until my companion stopped the car at a memorial, stating that it had been the site of a massacre following the Jacobite Rebellion in 1692. I have had this reaction many times since and I now recognize these places for what they are – traumatic imprints left on the land and calling out to be healed. You may well receive similar signals as you pass places of trauma. You can heal the land with the layout on page 121.

Repeating incidents

Repeating incidents at a site can be a signal that all is not well energetically. For example, a woman had a serious car accident alongside a bridge where her brother had been accidentally shot and killed, and her cousin badly injured in a crash. I wondered if her thoughts automatically went to her loss as she reached that spot. However, she said the bridge was known locally as a horror spot, because so many accidents and shootings had taken place there. When I tuned in, there was a very ancient ingrained destructive imprint at the site, which predated the bridge. Her brother, whose spirit was stuck at the site, was trying to get her attention; he had also been trying to get the attention of their cousin at the moment of the cousin's crash.

Crystals on a map dissolved the imprint and healed the horror, releasing her brother and several other souls who were trapped there. There can be many layers to such a healing and it may take years to heal them all, but one of the core processes is to bring forgiveness to the land and to the people concerned.

Dissolving an imprint

One way to dissolve an imprint that is not too firmly entrenched is to seed Halite crystals soaked in Petaltone Z14 essence into the earth in a Star of David pattern. This cleanses the energies. Then, place another Star of David at right angles to the first, this time seeded with Rhodochrosite or Rose Quartz on the points. This brings forgiveness and compassion. The results are a multi-dimensional energetic merkeba (a star tetrahedron composed of pyramids at right angles). You can expand the layout further if imprints are more deeply entrenched (see page 122).

Black Tourmaline, Brandenberg, Spirit and Smoky Quartz are all useful for dissolving an imprint in the land or moving on a lost soul.

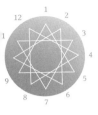

TRAUMA-CLEARING, FORGIVENESS AND RECONCILIATION LAYOUT

Layout: Double Star of David (see page 45)

Crystals: Black Tourmaline; Smoky Quartz; Rose Quartz; Rhodochrosite; Selenite (if the land has been cursed, place Purpurite in the centre); Rhodozite

Place this layout on a map or bury it. You can use other negativity-absorbing and forgiveness crystals if you prefer. Leave the layout to continue its work for as long as is needed. If souls are trapped at the site, see pages 122–3. Cleanse your crystals (see pages 19–21) and activate your dantien (see page 29) before you begin.

1   Hold your crystals in your hands for a few moments and state your intention that the layout dissolves the imprint, heals the land and brings forgiveness to the situation.
2   Lay a Black Tourmaline (negativity-absorbing) triangle on points 1, 5 and 9. Join up the triangle with your mind or a wand. Then, lay a Smoky Quartz (negativity-absorbing) triangle on points 3, 7 and 11. Join that triangle.
3   Lay a Rose Quartz (or other forgiveness crystal) on points 2, 6 and 10 and join the circuit. Then, lay a Rhodochrosite or other forgiveness crystal on points 4, 8 and 12. Join the circuit.
4   Place your hand over your heart and hold the intention that forgiveness and compassion be extended to all those involved (this is particularly potent if you have a personal connection to the event or to the site).
5   Put a large Selenite tower (or other light-bringing crystal, such as Purpurite for cursed sites) in the centre.
6   Place a Rhodozite circle all around the inside "circle" where the triangles intersect. This heals the land.
7   Leave the layout in place and cleanse it regularly (unless, of course, you have buried it in the ground).

SPIRIT RELEASE

Souls can easily become trapped at points of trauma in the landscape, or at places where leylines cross. Sometimes the passing over has been so fast that the person does not realize that their physical body has died and it is their soul body that they are inhabiting. At other times, strong emotions – such as anger or a desire for revenge – or unfinished business or a desire to have a proper burial can hold them fast between worlds, keeping the soul back from moving on. However, some souls contract to stay and guard a place – consider this option before moving spirits on.

Ghostly beings and stuck souls

Ghosts are imprints left behind on Earth, and they are rather different from stuck souls. Like a looped silent film, ghosts endlessly replay their past, "haunting" a place. They rarely harm others, but may create fear. Astral Clear from Petaltone essence placed on a Quartz crystal overnight usually dissolves them. This crystal remedy will also move a stuck soul on to the light, if the soul is ready to leave.

Stuck souls may not realize they are dead, as they *feel* alive. Some simply want to tell their story. Sometimes all that is needed is for them to recognize that time has moved on and they must move on, too. Some lost souls may be caught in an outdated viewpoint or intention. If you can hear their story and recognize how they could view it differently, they can see it through your eyes, which releases them. Although it is possible to assist lost souls using a crystal and your intuition, working with seriously troubled or malicious souls is best left to an expert.

If a group of spirits is trapped, lay out the trauma-clearing grid on page 121 and surround the layout with Smoky Spirit Quartz points facing inward. Hold the intention that the group be assisted to move to the light. Alternatively, you can use the process on the opposite page.

MOVING ON A LOST SOUL

Crystals: Black Tourmaline; Smoky Brandenberg or Smoky
Spirit Quartz

You will also need a candle. Find a quiet place where you will
be undisturbed, and cleanse your crystals (see pages 19–21)
and activate your dantien (see page 29) before you begin.

1   Programme a Black Tourmaline by holding it in your palm
    chakra and stating the intention that you want it to shield
    your energies. Wear it between your heart and throat.
2   Light a candle. Hold a Smoky Spirit Quartz or a Smoky
    Brandenberg in one hand, and focus on the intention that
    your inner eyes and ears be opened to communicate with
    the energies at the site.
3   Sit quietly and focus your attention on calling in higher
    helpers and guides to assist you. Open your heart and stay
    in a space of unconditional love and compassion.
4   Hold the intention that the spirit be taken to the light
    by his or her guardian angel or other helper. This works
    well if the spirit has simply lost the way home.
5   If the spirit is reluctant to move on and you are able to
    communicate, ask if there is anything you can do to assist.
    Requests are usually simple and often relate to unfinished
    business. Writing a spirit letter is helpful. You may achieve
    the spirit's release if you help the spirit to take a different
    view, particularly if you can help it to look back at how
    things were in the past and how they have changed.
6   Once the spirit has moved on, consciously disconnect
    and close your inner eyes and ears. Cleanse the crystals
    thoroughly before you put them away.

INTERDIMENSIONAL TRAVEL

Sometimes you will need to do the healing to restore the Earth's matrix grid from above the Earth to gain a more objective perspective or the wider viewpoint. Crystals facilitate your awareness leaving your body and travelling to a point in space from where you can see the globe with its energetic matrix grid turning below you as you undertake the healing.

Up, up and away

A combination of Preseli Bluestones and Anandalite™ facilitates journeying out of your body to the multi-dimensions that surround us. Lay the stones out around your body or on your chakras in the order that feels most appropriate for you, or sit in the middle of a circle of the stones and meditate on sending healing throughout the Earth's meridians to repair and reconstruct where necessary. You could also place the layout on the Earth's matrix grid or on Walter Bruneel's Earth Blessing mandala (see page 158). If you are new to crystal work, you may like to use a less potent Granite and Quartz combination until you get used to travelling through different dimensions. Always use an anchor stone such as Smoky Quartz or Smoky Elestial Quartz at your feet to bring you home to your physical body.

TRAVEL FACILITATOR

Placing a Preseli Bluestone over your soma chakra (see page 37) facilitates journeying out of your body. Place a large Smoky Quartz or Smoky Elestial at your feet to ensure your return and remember that the soma chakra has a cord attached to the subtle energy body in which you will make the journey. You can reel yourself back to your body via this cord.

MOVING-UPWARD LAYOUT

Layout: A straight line up the chakras (see page 32)

Crystals: Smoky Quartz or Smoky Elestial; Anandalite™ or Herkimer Diamonds and Preseli Bluestone (or Quartz and Granite for a lower-vibrational journey).

This layout works in conjunction with visualization. Usually, visualization means seeing pictures in your mind's eye, but you may not see images, you may have sensations or have to trust that the process is happening at another level. It can be helpful to imagine a screen onto which you project your pictures until you get the hang of stepping directly into the experience. Cleanse your crystals (see pages 19–21) and activate your dantien (see page 29) before you begin. (An alternative layout to the one below is to create a circle of crystals around you.)

1   Hold your crystals in your hands for a few moments to attune. State your intention of travelling through multi-dimensions to heal the Earth's matrix grid.
2   Place a Smoky Quartz or Smoky Elestial at your feet and picture it as an anchor stone to guide you back to your body.
3   Sit or lie comfortably (it is easier to place the stones if you lie down, but upward travel can be easier from sitting). Take your attention to your "third eye" (above and between your eyebrows). Feel this open like the petals of a flower.
4   Place Anandalite™ or Herkimer Diamond (or Quartz) as far as you can reach above your head. Place a Preseli Bluestone (or Granite) on your soma chakra (see page 37).
5   Feel yourself being drawn upward, passing swiftly through the walls above you and through the clouds above the Earth. You will pass through the planet's atmosphere and its many-layered etheric body, until you can see the globe turning beneath you.
6   Open your heart to the planet's fragile beauty.

Layout continues overleaf ▶

7 Allow your inner eye to open and perceive the Earth's matrix grid and its aura all around the globe. Note where it is broken, distorted or out of alignment and where the aura has detrimental imprints or holes, and use the power of the crystals to direct healing to bring the grid back into alignment and to repair the aura.

8 Feel the power flowing through all the lines equally bringing the planet back into equilibrium.

9 When the healing is complete, take your attention to the soma chakra and hold the intention that the Smoky Quartz at your feet draws you back down to your body. See the globe approaching and move toward your physical body.

10 Settle your awareness comfortably back within your body. Wriggle your fingers and toes. Close your third eye and remove the Preseli Bluestone from your soma chakra, and the Anandalite™ from above your head. Take a deep breath and open your eyes. Get up slowly. Stamp your feet on the ground to restore your connection to the Earth and ensure that your root chakra is open to hold you gently in your body, attached to the planet.

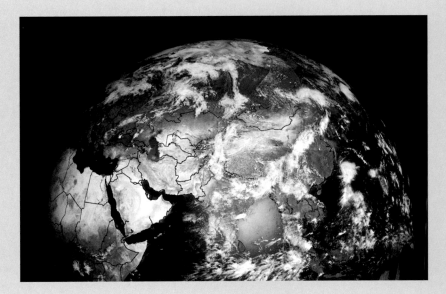

CALMING AREAS OF POLITICAL UNREST

You are watching the news on television. Scenes of violent protest and political upheaval unfold before your eyes. You feel powerless and helpless. You become anxious and distressed. What do you do? Reach for your crystals. The first stage is to centre and calm your own energies, and focus your intention into crystals programmed to help restore peace and order to the situation.

First-aid measures

As I have said before, in order to assist the Earth, it is important to keep your own energies high and clear. So, a piece of Rose Quartz or an Eye of the Storm held to your heart instantly calms you and sends unconditional love and peace to the scene of unrest.

However, this is not all you can do. Place your crystals on a map of the area to energetically defuse the situation and instil beneficial energy in place of negativity. When setting your intention, rather than asking for the outcome that you believe would be best, hold the intention for one that is for the highest good of all concerned. Sometimes the situation works out in unexpected ways or has a "healing crisis" – so don't panic if things seem to get worse before they get better. Hold the intention of the situation resolving itself and stay calm.

Practical application: not quite a revolution

In February 2013 I travelled with friends along the Nile in Upper Egypt, which was in turmoil (see "Light Becoming", www.judyhall.co.uk). The "Arab Spring" revolution had not brought the hoped-for changes; there was an economic crisis; and the people were suffering, especially in regions that rely so much on tourism. The plight of women was perilous – an English friend in Cairo was keeping us informed – and young men were disappearing. In addition, building the High Dam had changed the earth energies flowing down the Nile Valley and that, we believed, had had a long-term effect further up and down the river.

The whole land was uneasy and we needed to conduct a multi-layered healing. In Aswan Museum, which charts the history of Upper Egypt, we performed a soul retrieval for thousands of displaced souls from the drowned lands of Nubia. Outside the museum an archeoastronomer-earthworker energetically realigned the relocated stone circle and calendar avenue from Nabta Plya. When officials had first moved these sacred relics – the earliest known examples of their kind in the world – to the museum grounds, they had done so without reproducing their cosmic and earth-energy alignments.

At the High Dam, we stood over the river and, with my big Smoky Brandenberg Earth Healer and a clear, rainbow-filled Magnifier Record-keeper Quartz sent healing up and down the Nile and throughout the land. Our purpose was twofold: to heal the waters and also to bring the political situation to a resolution that was for the highest good of all.

We repeated the river healing at the Nilometer in Aswan itself. It was our intention that the river would then carry the healing downstream toward Egypt's capital itself.

However, some situations are rather like boils that need to be lanced – releasing the toxicity before they can heal. In July 2013, the death toll among protesters was rising and we heard that the army had taken over. Now back in England, I set up a grid over a map of Egypt, placing Eye of the Storm along key cities on the Nile, surrounding the boundaries of the country with Rose Quartz hearts. I also placed a large Eye of the Storm over Syria, Israel and Palestine to cover the unrest there. I added Golden Nubian temple stones from Aswan to the layout, and stabilized it with crystals of Smoky Elestial Quartz and a large Smoky Quartz point from Mount Sinai (a focal sacred site for the whole Middle East). I placed the layout on my dining-room table and every day I cleansed the crystals and renewed my intention that the situation would be resolved speedily and peacefully.

Making the layout work for you

The stones I used are appropriate for any situation of political turmoil. Lay the stones over key places in the relevant country and surround the borders with Rose Quartz hearts pointing inward. This channels the compassionate energy of these stones toward the capital city or the site of the unrest. If you have stones from the area, place these in the grid to strengthen the connection.

Eye of the Storm and Rose Quartz hearts laid along the Nile to bring peace; Rose Quartz hearts laid on the Egyptian border to surround the country with unconditional love.

HEALING THE BEES

We need bees and other pollinating insects to help sustain plant life – but they are constantly under threat from pollution and natural viruses. This layout channels healing energy to the bees.

SETTING OUT THE LAYOUT

Layout: Star of David (see page 45) or Flower of Life (see page 50)

Crystals: Bumble Bee Jasper; Smoky Brandenberg; Smoky Quartz (optional)

Cleanse your stones by placing them in brown rice overnight before using them, and activate your dantien (see page 29) before you begin. Note that you should wash your hands thoroughly after handling Bumble Bee Jasper as it contains toxic trace elements.

1 Hold the stones in your hands for a few moments stating your intention that they assist in healing the world's bees.

2 Set out your layout in the open air close to nectar-rich flowers, or use the template above and place a living flower next to it.

3 Lay out a photograph of a bee – this sets the intention that the bees need to be healed – and use the photograph as a base for your layout if you are using the Star of David. If you are using the Flower of Life, place the photograph to the side of the layout.

4 For the Star of David, place a downward-facing triangle of Bumble Bee Jasper to draw energy in toward the bee; and place an upward-facing triangle of Bumble Bee Jasper to radiate the energy out to all the bees and pollinating insects throughout the world. For the Flower of Life, lay out the stones in a pattern that intuitively feels right to you.

5 Place a Smoky Brandenberg in the centre to imprint
   the perfect etheric blueprint for maximum well-being.
6 Send out your wishes to heal the bees. Leave the layout
   in place for a few hours. (Place a Smoky Quartz at your
   feet if you feel at all floaty – it enables you to expand your
   consciousness and remain grounded at the same time.)

Making the layout work for you: the Flower of Life

If flowers do not grow where you live, you can place Bumble
Bee Jasper or Citrine on a Flower of Life and hold the intention
that this conveys healing to the bees and pollinating insects of
your neighbourhood, or to any domestic animals or wildlife that
need support.

Setting out the Healing the Bees layout near nectar-rich flowers
will enhance its effect.

Chapter Five

ESSENTIAL EARTH-HEALER CRYSTALS

All crystals assist in healing the Earth, it is their home after all, but I have specially chosen the selection here to give you a wide range of applications, frequencies and possibilities. They are the crystals in my own Earth-healing toolkit. It includes exceptionally high-vibration crystals, as well as those of a more earthy nature that ground the healing into the planet or your space. There are also crystals that help you to purify and stabilize your own personal energies. You won't need to buy them all: if you do not have a particular stone, you can use the energy embodied in the photograph in this chapter to do the healing work. Simply place your finger on the image of the crystal you wish to use to focus intention on that particular picture. Or, put the page face down and hold the intention that the crystal transfers its energy to your physical body, the environment or a map.

YOUR CRYSTAL TOOLKIT

An Earth-healing or space-clearing crystal toolbox benefits from having a range of stones in it, but you could use just one or two favourites if you so wish. I never travel without my big Smoky Brandenberg and a piece of local Flint. They, with the addition of Selenite and Golden or Clear Quartz, are all the tools I have needed in so many places around the world.

This directory is divided into two sections: the earthy healing stones that ground energy – and which may have a high vibration – and specifically high-vibration crystals that draw higher dimensional healing frequencies down to the Earth, but which may need anchoring.

"That mystic cave where the wise god a hoard
of all things good hath in his treasure stored.
He shall return, and bear in both his hands
A heap of blessings numerous as the sands."

The Lithica (lapidary, 4th century CE)

USING THE TOOLKIT

The toolkit on the following pages provides a directory of some of the crystals I most enjoy working with, a guide to their healing energies to help you with your own selections, and an opportunity for you to harness those energies using the photographs of the crystals when you don't have the crystals themselves. For each entry, I've listed where the crystal originates from, its associated chakras and its purpose.

THE EARTHY STONES

ARAGONITE

One of the most effective Earth-healing stones, Brown Aragonite grounds and stabilizes Earth's energy. Highly effective laid as a Pentangle (see page 46), it transforms geopathic stress and unblocks ley lines. Place it on a map to heal energetic disturbance or to restore equilibrium. Centring physical energies and calming over-sensitivity, it deepens your connection with the Earth, helping people with only a toehold in incarnation to feel that they belong. Aragonite facilitates insight into the causes of problems and assists with healing the ancestral line. Each colour works to a slightly different resonance: white purifies the vibrations, blue refines them, lilac reaches even higher and brown earths the contact. In layouts, Aragonite combines well with Black Tourmaline, Flint and Halite.

GEOGRAPHY Arizona (USA), Morocco, Namibia, New Mexico (USA), Spain, UK

CHAKRAS Resonates with the earth star and base chakras

PURPOSE To heal the Earth

GEOGRAPHY Afghanistan, Africa, Australia, Brazil, Germany, Italy, Madagascar, Sri Lanka, Tanzania, USA

CHAKRAS Resonates with the earth and base chakras; protects all

PURPOSE To protect from harm

GEOGRAPHY Indonesia, Northern Australia

CHAKRAS Resonates with the sacral and solar plexus chakras

PURPOSE To manifest the impossible

BLACK TOURMALINE

A powerful cleanser and purifier, Black Tourmaline draws negativity into the crystal, then locks it there so that it cannot escape. It is useful for creating a safe space in which to live and work. It absorbs electromagnetic pollution and geopathic stress, or ill-wishing. Placed on a map, it diffuses areas of tension. This stone encourages "positive neutrality", transforming ethnic or religious conflict into acceptance and assimilation.

BUMBLE BEE JASPER

Formed in the fumeroles of volcanoes and including a combination of Sulphur, Orpiment, Volcanic Ash and Anhydrite, Bumble Bee Jasper assists the impossible to manifest. Excellent for healing the bee population of the world (see page 131), it fertilizes possibilities on more subtle levels, too. Its vibrant colours infuse energy into the Earth and the physical body, and this bubbly stone can bring great joy to the user.

Note: Bumble Bee Jasper is toxic – handle it with care and wash your hands after using it.

GEOGRAPHY Worldwide

CHAKRAS Stimulates and cleanses all

PURPOSE To bring light and purity to the Earth

CLEAR QUARTZ

A master healing crystal, Quartz generates, releases, maintains and harmonizes energy at all levels. Place Quartz points into the earth as "acupuncture needles" that clear blockages and amplify the natural flow of energy around the planet's grid, bringing it back into equilibrium. You can also place large pieces of Quartz to maximize energy where needed. Clear Quartz is particularly useful when you need to encourage clarity and decisiveness.

CITRINE

Invigorating Citrine carries the energy of the sun and is an excellent stone for regeneration and abundance. Warming and creative, it radiates pure energy into the Earth's matrix grid. It assists people who are sensitive to environmental toxins and other outside influences. This crystal helps you develop a positive attitude, and to look forward instead of hanging onto the past. It encourages you to enjoy new experiences and explore every possibility; and it helps manifest the best solution to a problem. Kundalini Quartz (Natural Citrine from the Congo) bursts with kundalini energy and assists in raising Qi. Citrine is particularly effective in a counterclockwise Spiral on a map, as this links the energy of the sun to the heart of Mother Earth. Starting at the centre, it radiates energy outward. Starting on the outside, it pulls energy in.

GEOGRAPHY Brazil, Democratic Republic of the Congo, France, Madagascar, Russia, UK, USA

CHAKRAS Stimulates the solar plexus; purifies and aligns all

PURPOSE To bring the abundant light of the sun to the Earth

GEOGRAPHY South America

CHAKRAS Cleanses and aligns all
the chakras, particularly the heart

PURPOSE To maintain a point of
balance no matter what occurs

GEOGRAPHY Worldwide

CHAKRAS Stabilizes the earth
star and base chakras; cleanses all

PURPOSE To open a portal
to another world

EYE OF THE STORM
(JUDY'S JASPER)

A brand new find named by John
van Rees of Exquisite Crystals,
it should more properly be
called the "Eye of the Storm" as
holding it is like standing at the
epicentre of a storm – whirling
all around you while you remain
in a calm, centred space. The
crystal enables you to rise up
to obtain an objective view of
a situation. It is excellent for
stabilizing the Earth's grid and
calming areas of political unrest.
It can be programmed and left
in place for long periods of time.
This lovely stone has a beautiful,
heart-centred healing energy.

FLINT

An ancient Earth-healing stone
long seen as a portal to other
worlds, Flint stabilizes the Earth
and scours away negativity.
It assists shamanic journeying
through the underworld and the
caves and hidden crevasses of
the Earth for healing and soul
retrieval, or to repair energy
lines and to cast out dis-ease
and restore equilibrium. Flint
makes an excellent anchor for
grounding energy into a layout.

GEOGRAPHY Worldwide

CHAKRAS Cleanses and purifies all

PURPOSE To stabilize the Earth and the human energy field

GEOGRAPHY Madagascar, USA (as Zebra Stone)

CHAKRAS Cleanses and stabilizes all

PURPOSE To stabilize the Earth's meridians and bring them into equilibrium

GRANITE

High in Quartz and Feldspar, Granite is a strongly resonant, paramagnetic rock that generates and conveys a powerful current and acts like an acupuncture needle. Granite structures have a demonstrably higher radiation field around them. This stone releases blockages and ensures the smooth flow of Qi around the meridians of the Earth or the physical body. Granite stabilizes the human energy field, stimulating electrical activity in the cells and enhancing the immune system. It realigns the subtle bodies and creates a stable matrix for healing. The ancient Egyptians used Granite to draw the power of the gods to the Earth. It is an excellent gridding stone to create sacred space. Pink Aswan Granite facilitates reconnection to Egyptian temple lives and esoteric knowledge from that time.

GRAPHIC SMOKY QUARTZ (ZEBRA STONE)

Madagascan Smoky Quartz hugely compressed in a Feldspar matrix is invaluable when it comes to stabilizing layouts and realigning Earth energies, especially in areas where the ground has been under enormous pressure. As with all bi-coloured stones, Graphic Smoky Quartz promotes balance, stability and maturity, and helps to create an objective perspective. (It is also found in the USA where it is known as Zebra Stone.)

GEOGRAPHY Worldwide

CHAKRAS Cleanses all the chakras

PURPOSE To cleanse and purify

GEOGRAPHY Australia, Chile,
Democratic Republic of the Congo,
France, Germany, Middle East,
New Mexico (USA), Romania,
Russia, Zaire, Zambia

CHAKRAS Supports the base,
heart, sacral and solar plexus chakras

PURPOSE To dig deep and bring
up all that needs transmuting

HALITE

Halite is a cleansing stone that purifies an area and restores its balance. It assists in dissolving old patterns and ingrained feelings, no matter how ancient. Transmuting feelings of rejection or scapegoating, it increases goodwill. Halite stimulates the meridians of the physical body or the planet, and increases the healing properties of other crystals. Added to layouts, it draws off toxic energies.

MALACHITE

Malachite has a strong affinity with nature and with the devic forces that assist the self-regulating cycle of growth and decay. An important protection stone, it absorbs negative energies and electromagnetic pollutants easily, energetically absorbing them from the atmosphere or the earth and from the body. In particular, Malachite soaks up plutonium pollution, and guards against radiation of all kinds. Place it in homes near a nuclear or natural radiation source. It is a helpful stone for breaking old patterns and imprinting a new mind set.

Note: Use this stone in tumbled form and wash your hands after use.

GEOGRAPHY Africa, Australia, USA

CHAKRAS Unblocks the base
and sacral chakras

PURPOSE To promote fertility
and wisdom throughout the
stages of womanhood

MENALITE

Powerfully connected to Mother Earth
and the ancient fertility goddesses,
Menalite clears blockages from the
sacral and base chakras and takes you
back into the womb of Mother Earth for
healing and reconnection to the centre.
It solidifies your core energy field and
holds you gently in incarnation. Linking
to power animals, the Earth devas and
nature spirits, Menalite has long been
used to enhance rituals and shamanic
journeying, and to facilitate divination.
It reconnects you to feminine wisdom
and the power of the priestess. Useful
for rebirth and rejuvenation of any kind.

PRESELI BLUESTONE

Preseli Bluestone draws attention to
places where the Earth's grid needs
healing and where crystal intervention
would be helpful. Preseli Bluestone
"pegs" and knits together the lines on
the etheric planes, so that the healing
manifests in the physical. Preseli
Bluestone is strongly magnetic and
can realign the magnetic grid and
adjust anomalies. However, it may
also need to be aligned with the
Earth's north–south magnetic grid in
order to bring harmony – if you feel
uncomfortable when using it, turn
yourself and the stone until you
feel aligned. This stone helps you
to reconnect to your ancient Earth-
healing knowledge.

GEOGRAPHY Preseli Mountains,
Wales, and one small deposit
in Ireland

CHAKRAS Resonates with the
alta major, base and soma chakras

PURPOSE To facilitate shamanic
journeying and healing

GEOGRAPHY France, Namibia, Western Australia, USA

CHAKRAS Stimulates the crown chakra

PURPOSE To release anything that is blocked

GEOGRAPHY Rhodochrosite: Argentina, Peru, Romania, Russia, South Africa, Uruguay, USA; Perumar™: Peru

CHAKRAS Supports the heart and higher heart chakras; clears the base and solar plexus chakras

PURPOSE To instil love

PURPURITE

An excellent protection stone, Purpurite prevents psychic interference and shifts ingrained belief patterns. It removes curses and moves things on, imprinting positive energy. The stone stimulates spiritual insights and grounds the resultant energy shift into the Earth vibration.

RHODOCHROSITE AND PERUMAR™ (BLUE RHODOCHROSITE)

A stone of compassion and selfless love, Rhodochrosite expands consciousness and integrates new information into the material world. Rhodochrosite helps you to face the truth without judgment, revealing the part you played in creating situations. It gently heals the past, releasing toxic emotions and experiences, and imparts a positive attitude to life. It encourages giving service to the planet and all those upon it. Gentle, blue Perumar™ links to the wisdom of the Incas and their sacred sites high in the Andes mountains. The stone has tiny flaws to remind us to forgive and have compassion for imperfections in our own character and in that of others. It encourages a positive view of the future and assists the Earth's kundalini to settle into its new orientation along the Andes.

GEOGRAPHY Madagascar, USA

CHAKRAS Cleanses and revitalizes all

PURPOSE To heal the Earth

RHODOZITE

Although tiny, Rhodozite is an extremely powerful Earth healer, especially when placed onto maps. It enhances the effects of other crystals. As it rarely needs cleansing, Rhodozite can simply be left to do its work. Reputedly the Madagascan shamans favour this stone for weather magic – try placing it to calm inclement conditions. This highly energetic stone can add vitality to the physical body or the planet as it enhances the flow of Qi through the meridians.

Note: Rhodozite in Feldspar accelerates the effect and grounds the energy into the Earth.

GEOGRAPHY Brazil, Germany, India, Japan, Madagascar, South Africa, USA

CHAKRAS Resonates with the heart, higher heart and heart seed chakras

PURPOSE To bring universal love and peace to the Earth

ROSE QUARTZ

Crystallized love, serene Rose Quartz infuses peace and harmony, calming areas of unrest and restoring balance. It is the ultimate forgiveness stone. Rose Quartz resonates with Archangel Ariel, who watches over the Earth. Meditate with this stone to project peaceful thoughts around the world, or place it in a layout for prolonged Earth regeneration and healing.

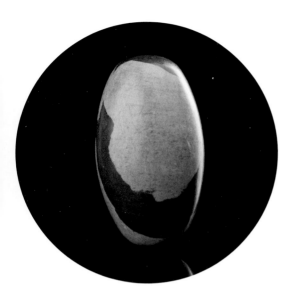

GEOGRAPHY The bed of
the Narmada River, India

CHAKRAS Resonates with all,
but especially the base, earth
star and sacral chakras

PURPOSE To purify and sanctify
a space and write dualities

SHIVA LINGAM

According to ancient lore, the cryptocryastalline Quartz matrix
from which a Shiva Lingam is formed was created when a
meteorite hit the planet, uniting Earth and sky. The red markings
are meteoric iron and the stones also contain Chalcedony, Goethite,
Agate and Basalt. A stone of soul awareness collected from the
bed of the Narmada River, a Shiva Lingam can be implanted into
the Earth's acupuncture points or set up as an altar – these stones
purify and sanctify your home. A cosmic and etheric amplifier, a
Lingam is imbued with vitality and Qi, and stimulates the kundalini
of the Earth or the physical body. It activates all the chakras,
both human and global. Enhancing a sense of community and
forgiveness, a Lingam brings about unity in the face of diversity,
separation or conflict. It facilitates transformation by breaking up
old patterns and opening a path to a new life. Traditionally used
to enhance fertility, the stone assists in feeling comfortable in
incarnation. This stone of divine creative manifestation symbolizes
the dance of the cosmos and its polarities: the interplay of *yin* and
yang, body and soul – the inner and outer processes that hold the
planet and the human body in perfect balance. Lingams carry the
elemental energies of earth, water, wind and fire. Rare black Basalt
Shiva Lingams are highly protective.

GEOGRAPHY Worldwide

CHAKRAS Resonates with the base and earth star chakras

PURPOSE To ground and cleanse (one of the most efficient stones for this purpose)

GEOGRAPHY South Africa

CHAKRAS Cleanses and unifies all

PURPOSE To unite

SMOKY QUARTZ

An excellent earthing and purifying stone, Smoky Quartz soaks up negative energies and transmutes them. It anchors a layout while at the same time raising the vibrations of the surrounding area. Smoky Quartz blocks geopathic stress and stimulates insights and Earth healing. Assisting in moving between alpha and beta states of mind, it facilitates journeying with awareness.

SPIRIT QUARTZ

Spirit Quartz radiates high-vibration energy, while the core tightly focuses healing that reaches multi-dimensions, and reprograms cellular memory. It cleanses other stones and stabilizes earth energy in a healing layout. This stone takes you to meet the ancestors and you can program it for ancestral healing. Extremely beneficial in past-life healing, it pinpoints the gift or karmic justice in traumatic situations, promotes self-forgiveness and balances male and female energies. Citrine Spirit Quartz releases dependence on material things. It heals disturbed earth energies, helps to resolve conflict and sends forgiveness. Amethyst Spirit Quartz transmutes misuses of spiritual power, gently dissolving karma and toxic attitudes. Smoky Spirit is strongly protective, grounding and cleansing. It facilitates spirit-release work, or exploring the subconscious, and stabilizes environmental imbalance or pollution.

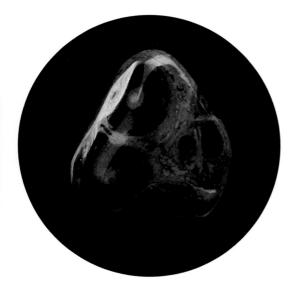

GEOGRAPHY Australia, Madagascar, Russia, USA

CHAKRAS Stabilizes all

PURPOSE To learn from experience

STROMATOLITE AND KAMBABA JASPER (GREEN STROMATOLITE)

The fossilized remains of one of the most ancient of lifeforms, Kambaba Jasper (Green Stromatolite) and Stromatolite are strongly earthing, reconnecting you to Mother Earth and the Earth devas. Stromatolite attunes you to – and reharmonizes – the deeper cycles and rhythms of the planet and the natural world, realigning your personal biorhythm to that of Earth. Going right to the foundations to create stability – physical and of purpose – it is particularly beneficial for the lungs, both human and planetary. Stromatolite supports photosynthesis in plants and increases oxygen output. Place this stone where you need to draw in more oxygen or to transmute excess carbon dioxide. An excellent support during evolutionary change, having existed throughout billions of years of chaos, catastrophe and transformation, it instils the ability to "let go" or to opt out without compromising your integrity. Lay the stone out on the ground or on a map to repair and activate the Earth's meridians, and to improve fertility in the earth, as well as the physical body. Stromatolite acts as a portal to the far past of the Earth, delving deep into its history and evolution so that it can take you back to heal the past or to bring forward ancient knowledge, opening evolutionary portals that were set in place in previous civilizations.

GEOGRAPHY India, but increasingly available elsewhere

CHAKRAS Cleanses all; activates the higher crown chakra in particular

PURPOSE To facilitate spiritual evolution

GEOGRAPHY Namibia

CHAKRAS Realigns and activates all

PURPOSE To return the world to perfection

THE HIGH-VIBRATION CRYSTALS

ANANDALITE ™
(AURORA QUARTZ)

Iridescent, rainbow-coated Anandalite™ (Aurora Quartz) has exceptionally high vibrations and carries powerful bioscalar healing waves and abundant Qi. It is an amazing crystal to work with for personal or Earth healing. The crystal knows exactly what to do, all you have to do is attune to it for a few moments and intuitively follow its instructions. Sweeping it from the feet to above the head and back down to the feet cleanses and activates all the chakras and enhances spiritual awareness.

BRANDENBERG

A Brandenberg carries the original core spiritual blueprint *and its highest potential*. It heals a personal bioenergetic field or the Earth's biosphere and etheric grid. Raising vibrations, it shields background psychic interference. Smoky Brandenberg removes implants, attachments, spirit possession or mental influence. It assists conscious transformation. A gatekeeper, Smoky Brandenberg also protects against psychic attack, repelling negative energy and calling in positive vibes. The crystal shifts ingrained past-life trauma and heals soul splits whether personal or in the earth.

GEOGRAPHY Brazil (a thermally shocked Brazilian high-vibration Quartz)

CHAKRAS Energizes and aligns all, but especially the higher chakras

PURPOSE To fertilize the Earth with the light of the sun

"FIRE AND ICE" (RAINBOW QUARTZ)

A light-bringer and high-resonance Quartz, Fire and Ice Quartz has many fractures, flaws and inclusions within it, creating numerous rainbows and linking to higher consciousness. Having been thermally shocked, this is a stone for new beginnings and profound growth, cutting through the old self to ignite the soul's purpose. Carrying cosmic fire and with power to fertilize the earth, Fire and Ice acts as a battery for the Earth's grid. Drawing light from the sun, it transmits it into the pulsating heart of Mother Earth, repairing the Earth's energy grid, infusing the crystal matrix with Qi, and seeding the formation of new crystals. Fire and Ice aligns with the Andes, where the kundalini flow now lies north to south, and has a particular resonance with the heart chakra of that mountain line.

Note: If Fire and Ice is not available, use Quartz with plenty of inclusions and rainbows to capture the energy of the sun.

GEOGRAPHY The most potent Golden Healer Quartz – the Nubian Temple Stones – come from the Aswan area and Nile flood plain. Other stones are found worldwide, especially in the mountain ranges of the USA.

CHAKRAS Aligns and activates all, but especially the higher chakras

PURPOSE To bring Christ Consciousness to the Earth

150

GOLDEN HEALER QUARTZ

Found in several forms, ranging from transparent to milky, Golden Healer Quartz, with its high iron content, has an extremely active vibration and is suitable for all sacred and healing space. Creating immense peace, it is often found around sacred sites as water-worn opaque pebbles, like the Nubian Temple Stones; or laid down in layers, such as potent Rainbow Mayanite. It contains a high ratio of Qi and bioscalar waves that create a multidimensional healing layout around a site or the planet, or between the cells of the physical body. Carrying Christ Consciousness, it acts as a catalyst for profound spiritual growth. Golden Healer purifies and re-energizes the chakras, rapidly releasing toxic mental or emotional conditioning.

GEOGRAPHY True Herkimers: Herkimer County, USA. Arkansas Diamonds, Himalayan Herkimers and similar Quartzes available elsewhere

CHAKRAS Clears and aligns all; activates the third eye chakra

PURPOSE To transmute negativity into positive evolution

GEOGRAPHY Austria, England, France, Germany, Greece, Mexico, Poland, Russia, Sicily, USA

CHAKRAS Activates all, especially the higher chakras

PURPOSE To bring light to the world

HERKIMER DIAMONDS

Essential for layouts in areas of electromagnetic or geopathic stress or disturbed earth energy, Herkimers block negativity and transmute it to positivity. A layout of Herkimers clears the chakras in minutes. Smoky Herkimers are excellent healing stones for both your own root (earth) chakra and the Earth itself. The yellow ("Citrine") ones are brilliant cleansers and regenerators, especially when they contain oil from the Himalayas or iron (Golden Herkimers). They are excellent for restoring vitality.

Note: You can substitute Arkansas Diamonds and similar Quartzes if necessary.

SELENITE

Crystallized divine light, Selenite infuses that light into the Earth's matrix grid and the hearts of all those who live on the planet. Translucent white Selenite is said to inhabit the place between light and matter, bringing a new vibration to the Earth. It is particularly effective placed in a protective layout around a house. A large piece placed in the earth ensures a peaceful atmosphere. Selenite disintegrates when wet so do replace it from time to time.

GEOGRAPHY Worldwide, but Brazil in particular

CHAKRAS Purifies all; particularly beneficial for the earth star chakra

PURPOSE To raise the vibration of the Earth

GEOGRAPHY Brazil

CHAKRAS Activates all

PURPOSE To revitalize the Earth and all those upon it

SMOKY ELESTIAL QUARTZ

A higher vibration of Smoky Quartz. With its many folds and facets and its Earth angel and devic connections, Smoky Elestial Quartz is particularly useful in Earth healing as it not only absorbs and transmutes negativity, but also raises the vibration of the Earth at the same time. This is an excellent protection, transmutation and journeying stone that can be left in place for long periods. Place it on the earth star chakra to activate and ground a connection to the earth.

TANGERINE DREAM LEMURIANS

These Lemurians pack a powerful punch. Full of lifeforce, they re-energize depleted energy and shift ingrained patterns, opening blocked potential. The quickest way to effect a shift is to place them over an area on a map in a star burst. Tangerine Dream Lemurians open a portal to expanded soul healing. All Lemurians open an energy portal to stellar experiences, anchoring ancient wisdom into the present. Attuning to spiritual training and initiations, Lemurians reawaken inherent skills and healing abilities. Combine them with Smoky Elestials to anchor high-vibration energy.

Note: If Tangerine Dream Lemurian is not available, use Tangerine, Apricot or Golden Quartz points instead.

GEOGRAPHY Trigonic Quartz: Brazil; Trigonic markings are appearing on other crystals worldwide

CHAKRAS Opens the higher crown chakras

PURPOSE To remove war from our planet

TRIGONIC QUARTZ

The soul midwife stone that carries cosmic consciousness, Trigonic Quartz holds a hologram of all potentiality and links to the Akashic Record. It settles a new pattern into the Earth rather than creating a fresh one, so you may need to incorporate other stones, such as Brandenberg, Herkimers or Smoky Elestial, into layouts intended to transform an outdated pattern or to input a more beneficial one. When using a Trigonic for personal layouts, do not point directly at the top of your head as it will disrupt your energies instead of raising them. Align the stone precisely so that it passes above the head and through the soul star or stellar gateway. This stone makes you go with the flow and stay with what is. It shows you where you are not aligned with your core soul purpose. Trigonic has an innate connection with water and powerful water-healing properties.

APPENDIX

State stones, national crystals and archangel connections

A country or national stone supports the energy of that country. Such connections can be incorporated into Earth-healing layouts, whether placed on the actual ground or on a map. Many crystals also have traditional archangel, saint or day-of-the-week links – you can invoke these to assist with healing.

Agate
States: Kentucky, Louisiana, Maryland, Minnesota, Montana, Nebraska, New York, Oregon, South Dakota, Tennessee
Countries: Denmark, Panama
Connections: Shekinah, Archangel Michael

Ajoite
State: Arkansas
Country: South Africa
Connections: All archangels

Amber
Countries: France, Romania, Sicily

Amethyst
State: South Carolina
Country: Uruguay
Connections: St Valentine, Thursday, Apostles Judas and Matthew, Archangel Raphael

Amphibole Quartz
Connection: Archangel Gabriel

Aragonite
Country: Spain
Connection: Mother Earth

Beryl
State: New Hampshire
Connections: Apostle Thomas, Archangels Auriel and Zadkiel, Angelic Dominions

Carnelian
Countries: Norway, Sweden

Celestite
State: Pennsylvania
Connections: Blue Celestite: Archangel Michael; "Lilac Celestite" (Lilac Anhydrite): Zadkiel

Cinnabar
Connections: Archangel Michael, Wednesday

Danburite
State: Connecticut
Connection: Angelic Realm

Diamond
Countries: England, Netherlands, South Africa
Connections: Hindu gem for April, Archangel Metatron, Sunday

Emerald
State: North Carolina
Countries: Peru, Spain
Connections: Hindu gem for May, Apostle John, Archangel Ophaniel, Cherubim, Friday

Flint
State: Ohio

Garnet
States: Alaska, Connecticut (Almandine Garnet), Idaho (Star Garnet), Vermont (Grossular Garnet)
Country: former Czechoslovakia
Connections: Apostle Andrew, Archangels Zadkiel and Michael, Thrones, Tuesday

Granite
States: New Hampshire, North and South Carolina, Wisconsin, Vermont

Hematite
State: Alabama

Iolite
Connections: Archangels Gabriel and Michael

Jade
States: Alaska, Wyoming
Countries: New Zealand, Turkestan

Jasper
Connections: Angelic Principalities,
Apostle Peter, Archangels Haniel
and Sandalphon

Labradorite
State: Oregon
Connection: Saturday

Lapis Lazuli
Countries: Bolivia, Chile, Bukhara
(Uzbekistan)
Connection: Archangel Michael

Moonstone
State: Florida
Connections: Archangel Gabriel,
Monday

Morganite (Pink Beryl)
Country: Madagascar

Obsidian
Country: Mexico

Black Fire Opal
States: Nevada, New South Wales
Country: Hungary

Peridot
Country: Egypt
Connections: Angelic Virtues, Apostle
Bartholomew, Archangel Raphael,
Saturday

Petrified Wood
States: Alberta, Mississippi,
Washington

Quartz
States: Arkansas, Georgia, Iowa
Country: Switzerland

Rhodochrosite
State: Colorado

Rhodonite
State: Massachusetts
Country: Russia

Rose Quartz
State: South Dakota
Connections: January

Ruby
Countries: Myanmar, Thailand
Connections: Hindu gem for August;
Apostle Jude, Tuesday

Sapphire
State: Montana (Montana Sapphire)
Country: USA
Connections: Apostle Andrew,
Archangels Metatron and Zadkiel,
St Paul, Seraphic Realm

Seraphinite
Connection: Archangel Raphael

Serpentine
States: California, Rhode Island

Smoky Quartz
State: New Hampshire
Country: Scotland
Connection: 1am

Sugilite
Connection: Archangel Michael

Sunstone
State: Oregon

Topaz
State: Texas (Blue Topaz), Utah
(Yellow Topaz)
Connections: Hindu gem for
December, Apostles James the Less
and Matthew, Archangels in general
and specifically Michael and Raziel,
Cherubim, Sunday

Tourmaline
States: Maine, New England
Country: Brazil
Connection: Wednesday

Turquoise
States: Arizona, Nevada, New Mexico
Country: Turkey, Iran
Connections: Thursday, fifth hour of
the day

Zincite
Country: Poland

GLOSSARY

Aura: the organized, subtle biomagnetic sheath that surrounds the physical body and the Earth

Biomagnetic: the magnetic field created by a living organism, or the effect of a magnetic field on an organism

Bioscalar waves: a standing energy field created when two electromagnetic fields counteract each other. It directly influences tissue at the microscopic level, bringing about healing balance. Bioscalar waves support cell membranes in manifesting the most beneficial genetic potential. They enhance the immune and endocrine systems, improve the coherence of the biomagnetic field and support healing at all levels.

Biosphere: all the Earth's ecosystems as a single, self-sustaining unit

Cellular memory: the memory within cells of previous or ancestral attitudes, trauma and patterns that have become deeply ingrained as on-going negative programs that create dis-ease or are replayed in the present in slightly different forms

Chakra: an energy linkage point between the physical and subtle bodies. Malfunction leads to physical, emotional, mental or spiritual dis-ease or disturbance.

Crystal oversouls: Michael Eastwood's name for beings that inhabit crystals and work from other dimensions. These beings communicate across space, time and distance and hold keys to our evolution that are activated when we make contact with the oversouls via the crystals.

Devas: nature and other spirits who care for the Earth

Earth healing: rectifying the distortion of the Earth's energy field or meridian grid caused by pollution, electromagnetic interference and the destruction of its resources

Electromagnetic smog: a subtle but detectable electromagnetic field given off by power lines and electrical equipment that has an adverse effect on sensitive people

Etheric body: a subtle counterpart to the physical body that surrounds and interpenetrates it

Geopathic stress: earth and physiological stress resulting from subtle emanations and energy conflicts or disturbances from underground water, power lines, natural landscape features, negative earth energy and other subterranean events

Grid: the energetic geomagnetic templates encompassing the Earth that create a matrix around and interpenetrating it

Grounding: creating a strong connection between one's soul, physical body and the Earth

Journeying: the experience of consciousness leaving the physical body and travelling to distant locations

Kundalini: inner, subtle spiritual and sexual energy that resides at the base of the spine and, awakened, rises to the crown chakra. Kundalini is also found in the Earth.

Layout: placing crystals in a pattern around a building, person or place for energy enhancement or protection

Magnifier: A crystal with a twist that amplifies and enhances energies and intent; what Robert Simmons calls a "vibrational turbo-charger"

Matrix: the bedrock on which crystals are formed. An energetic matrix also interpenetrates the planet.

Mental influences: effect of people's thoughts and strong opinions on your mind or on the planet

Meridian: a subtle energy channel that runs close to the surface of the skin or of the globe

Psychogeology: Richard Allen's term for the interplay between geology and human beings; how mind is shaped by geological processes

Qi: the life force that energizes the subtle and physical bodies and the planet

Subtle energy fields: invisible but detectable energy fields that surround all living beings

Sacred landscape: a place that evokes the sacred and resonates with our deeper selves

Self-healed: a crystal that has been cracked or fractured and that "grows" small points on the broken face

Spirit release: facilitating trapped or troubled spirits leaving the Earth-plane, releasing them to move to other dimensions

Telluric: energies generated by the Earth

Tumbled: a stone that has had its rough edges removed and its surface polished

Vortex: a whirling energy portal that may be electric, magnetic or electromagnetic. Strictly speaking the plural is vortices, but in earth-energy terms they are known as vortexes.

RESOURCES

Crystals
High-vibration crystals, Earth healers and other crystals specially charged up for you by Judy Hall are available from **www.angeladditions.co.uk**

Trigonics, Eye of the Storm (Judy's Jasper) and just about everything else can be obtained from John van Rees at **www.exquisitecrystals.com**

Cleansing and recharging
Petaltone crystal cleansing and recharging essences and Astral Clear: **www.petaltone.co.uk**

Crystal Balance cleansing and recharging essences: **www.crystalbalance.net**

For further information
For details of psychogeology see: **www.psychogeology.net**
Earth-healing mandalas, visionary art, dragon wisdom and angelic beings are all explained at: **www.walterbruneel.com**
Spirit Release Foundation: **www.spiritrelease.com**
School of Intuition and Healing: **www.intuitionandhealing.co.uk**

Further reading
By Judy Hall
– *Crystal Bible*, Volumes 1, 2 and 3, Godsfield (London, 2003/2009, 2009, 2013)
– *The Crystal Experience*, Godsfield (London, 2010)
– *The Crystal Wisdom Oracle*, Watkins (London, 2013)
– *Crystals and Sacred Sites*, Fair Winds Press (London, 2012)
– *Life-Changing Crystals*, Godsfield (London, 2013)
– *101 Power Crystals*, Fair Winds Press (London, 2011)
– *Crystal Practicalities* – DVD or download from **www.angeladditions.co.uk**

Other good reads
Coon, Robert, Earth Chakras website, www.earthchakras.org
Pasichnyk, Richard, *In Defense of Nature*, Writers Club Press (Lincoln, NE, 2002)
– *The Vital Vastness*, Volumes 1 and 2, Writer's Showcase (Lincoln, NE, 2002)

INDEX

Author acknowledgments My love and thanks to the photographers Michael Illas, Jeni Campbell, Terrie Birch and Page Amber Smith for capturing the energies and layouts so well. To Tania Ahsan my gratitude for believing in the project and to Fiona Robertson for carrying it through. The designer Allan Sommerville and editor Judy Barratt helped me to shape the book and brought it to fruition. And to the lovely crystal suppliers who have introduced me to some wonderful crystals over the years, my deepest blessings. Thanks also to Walter Bruneel for creating his amazing mandalas and allowing me to use them, and to John van Rees of www.exquisitecrystals.com for his good sense, humour and, most of all, his incredible stones.

The author and publishers would like to thank all those who have given permission to reproduce their copyright material. Every care has been taken to trace copyright owners, but if we have omitted anyone we apologize and will, if informed, make corrections in any future edition.

Picture credits All images Michael Illas © Watkins Publishing except pages 15 BRGM, France via OneGeology Maps; 43 Jeni Campbell; 67 via Healing Humanity; 78 Jeni Campbell; 81 Jeni Campbell; 91 Terrie Birch; 96 Jeni Campbell; 97 Jeni Campbell; 98 Jeni Campbell; 99 Jeni Campbell; 118 Page Amber Smith; 126 MarcelClemens/ Shutterstock; 131 Jeni Campbell.